Verlag der Buchhandlung Walther König

Bu kitaba önsöz yazarken
ölüm haberini aldığım dayım
Köksal
ve
daha önce kaybettiğimiz kardeşleri
Kenan ve Sinan ikizlerin
güleryüzlü hatıralarına.

To the genial memory of
uncle Köksal,
who passed away
when I was working on the preface
of this book,
and also to his brothers
Kenan and Sinan twins.

Table of Contents

doesn't talk about what this book is about.

And this book does not attempt to comprehensively explain the works that are featured in it. Variations of works, studies or parts of series (i.e. *Rulers*) are not fully featured.

Room of Rhythms 1 aims to introduce or reestablish the primary visual components of works and studies, mostly by providing a single image and simple caption information. The conversation, which stands as the only text except for this preface, helps arrange and reintroduce a part of the visuals, in addition to transmitting bits of conceptual background, description and history. It is literally a conversation, even though it is edited and modified. It flows by instantly using its own record.

On April 25, 2012, we recorded a conversation, mostly a straightforward Q&A, in a little more than 2 hours. Duygu transcribed and translated this dialogue and sent it to me. We went over it a few times, took out some things, and added others. As mentioned above: It comprises the main text of this book and allows us to include selected visual documentation of the works that are mentioned intentionally and sometimes strategically, as well as other related images, creating a visual sequence.

I would like to list a few things that led to the formation of this book:

- The natural desire to leave a tangible trace of the work that is done. We had already spent some time compiling information on the work with the goal of making a document.

- In 2005, *Studio* (see images on p.43 and p.66-67) was awarded the W.F.C. Uriôt prize at Rijksakademie, which triggered the making of this book. After attempts at making a book in 2006 and then again in 2007 (you can see some traces of this effort on p.43, a panoramic view planned as a fold-out); it turned out that I wasn't going to be able to undertake the making of this book yet (I didn't know at all what kind of book it was going to be). The works, most of which are included in this book, were still (and will be) taking shape, and it didn't seem feasible at the time. I explained this to the academy, and they understandingly accepted, postponing the project to a further date. I would like to take this opportunity to thank them for not allowing the prize to expire in these 7 years. Especially to Tinie Kerseboom, then Head of Publications, for her patience with my "there-is-no-hurry-for-a-publication" behavior, and to Martijntje Hallmann, Head of Ateliers, for her continuous support, and all the others at Rijksakademie who were directly or indirectly involved with what I tried to do while I was there.

- Earlier this year, Carolyn Christov-Bakargiev, the artistic director of dOCUMENTA (13), came to see my exhibition *Week*, which took place at Kunsthalle Basel, and to discuss the work, the space, and what I planned for *Room of Rhythms* at dOCUMENTA (13) in Kassel. It was a nice and productive meeting, after which Adam Szymczyk, the director of Kunsthalle Basel, joined us while we were having a fast meal and reminded us of my idea for a book. To be honest, in my excitement about the installation I was on the verge of pushing it to the back of my head once more, as I had done for many years.

Carolyn determinedly and instantly followed up on our conversation and
facilitated the collaboration with Walther König. I would like to thank Carolyn,
Adam as well as Franz König and Hanna Schmandin of Walther König, who
all took part in creating a chain reaction, from initiating the process to seeing
this fast sequence of events take shape, culminating in this book. I would like
to express my gratitude to designer Sabine Pflitsch and probsteibooks, to whom
I was introduced by König, and who made the physicality of the book possible
with their efficient but warm way of working, mostly communicating online.
At the risk of this becoming a thank-you list, I would also like to thank everyone and every institution who supported the book and the works that are
included in it, whom I am not able to mention by name here.

I would like to add a few words about why I took on the job of making this
book together with Duygu Demir (or why Duygu undertook the task of making
it with me). She is the person best acquainted with the archival totality of the
work I have done, not only in terms of date, title, place, version and images,
but also in terms of stories and adventures experienced or made up by me that
relate to the work. This familiarity is because we have worked together since
2009 on a documentation effort; which, first unknowingly, and later intentionally, formed the basis of this book. I would like to thank her for co-composing,
co-organizing, translating, editing, re-editing and steering the wheel during the
process, performing a wide range of tasks under the "editor" title.

The preparation process for this book and the outcome helped me remember
and reconsider past work, during a time period that spanned several stages of a
new work in progress. This work in progress, which has the same title as the
book and is mentioned repeatedly in it, is now born and already has its own
life at dOCUMENTA (13). I can say that the formation process of the book very
successfully fulfilled its aim in helping me re-visit and consult previous experi-
ences while taking them a step further.

And a note about the "1" that follows *Room of Rhythms* in the title: Yes, I
would like this book that is comprised of images, a brief conversation and
rough technical information to continue, to evolve into a series. There is so
much to talk about, to document, to refer to or to propose. Alas, the work
continues. Rhythms, spaces and the life in and around them continue.
Can a book on them end? Not at all. (This can be considered a wink to the
publisher.) The first follow-up idea that comes to mind is to have Volume 2
focus on the conception and realization of what gave this book its title:
Room of Rhythms at dOCUMENTA (13); perhaps the second one would
contain sounds... perhaps.

Cevdet Erek, Istanbul and Kassel, July 2012

   Video stills from *1:86400*, 2003

16:09
21 07
2003

Pazartesi
Montag
Monday

Salı
Dienstag
Tuesday

Çarşamba
Mittwoch
Wednesday

Pe
Do
Th

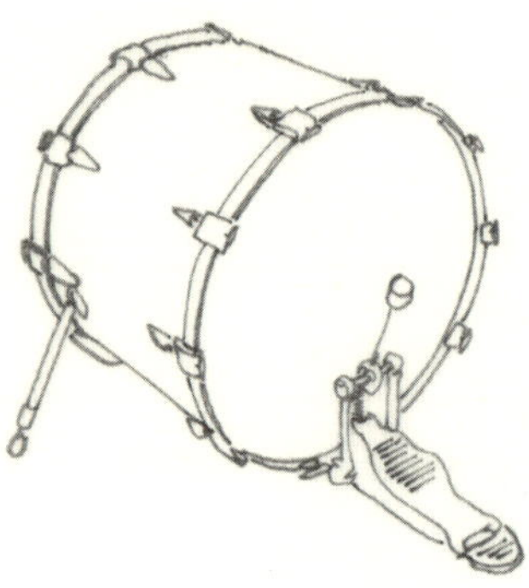
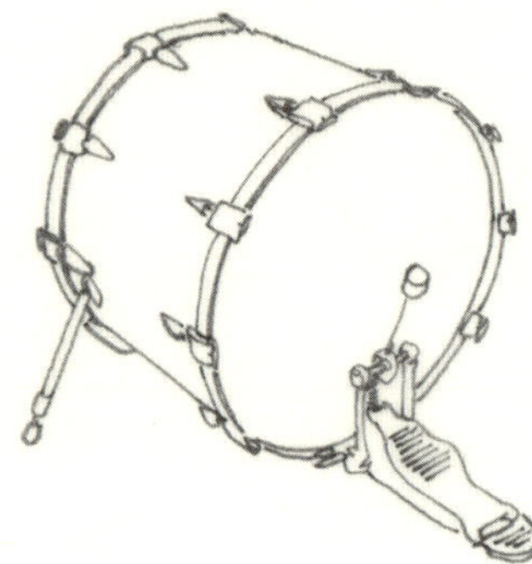
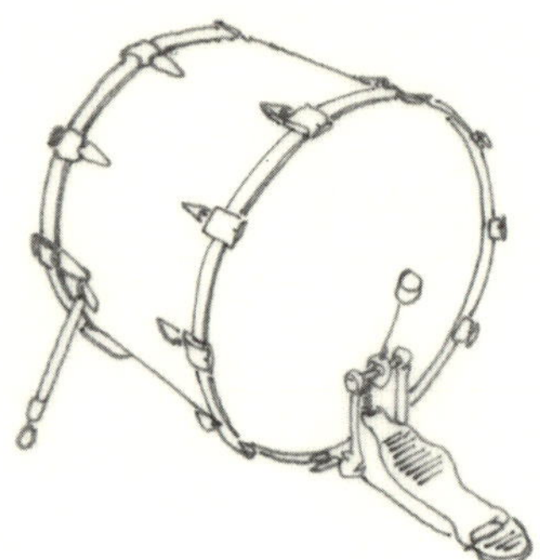
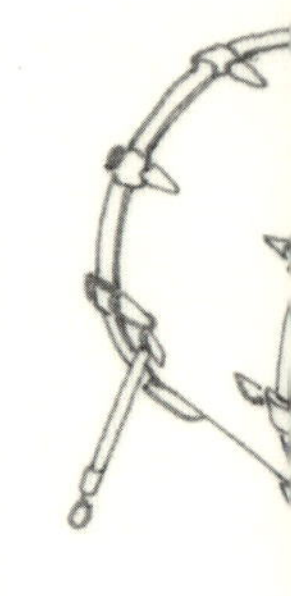

Pazartesi
Montag
Monday

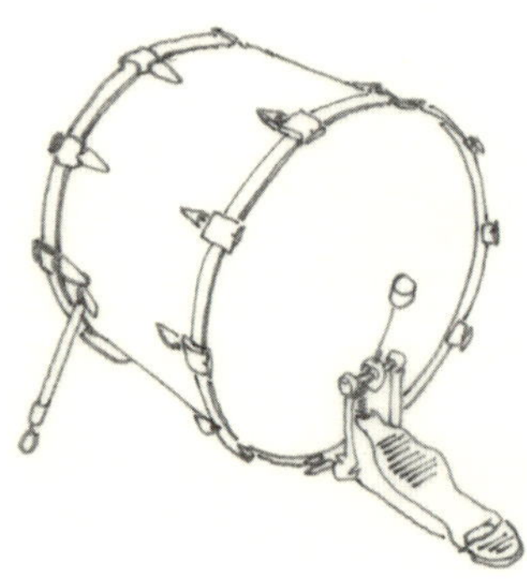

  Notation for sound piece of *Week*, as printed in booklet, Kunsthalle Basel, 2012

Cuma
Freitag
Friday

Cumartesi
Samstag
Saturday

Pazar
Sonntag
Sunday

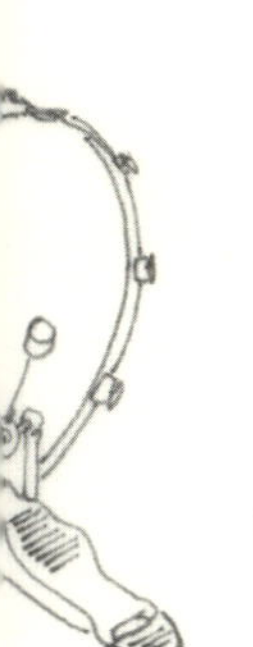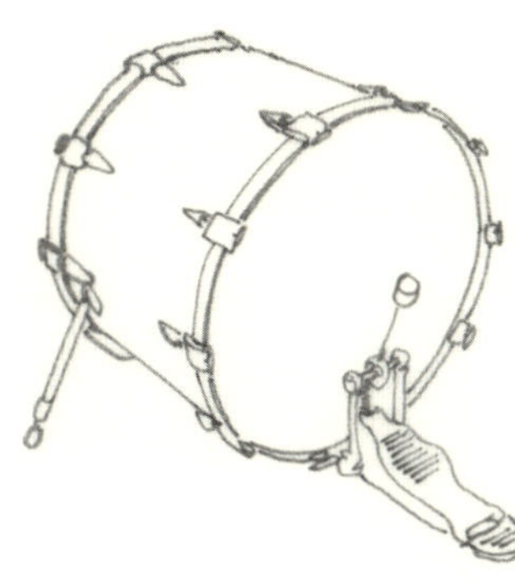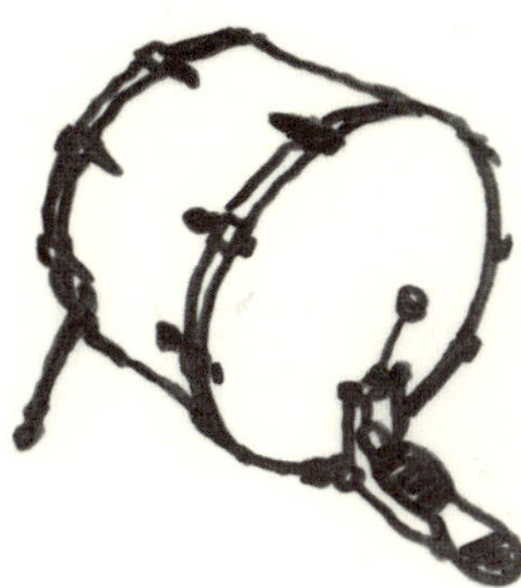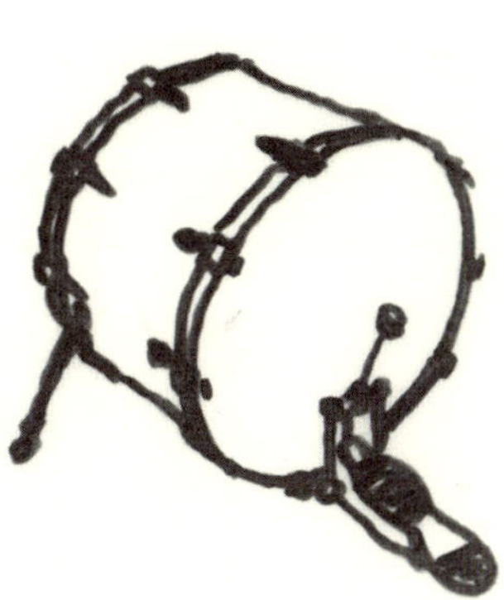

Hafta sonu
Wochenende
Weekend

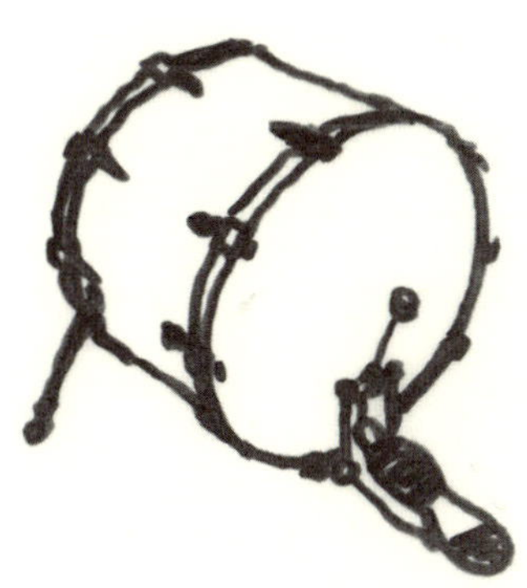

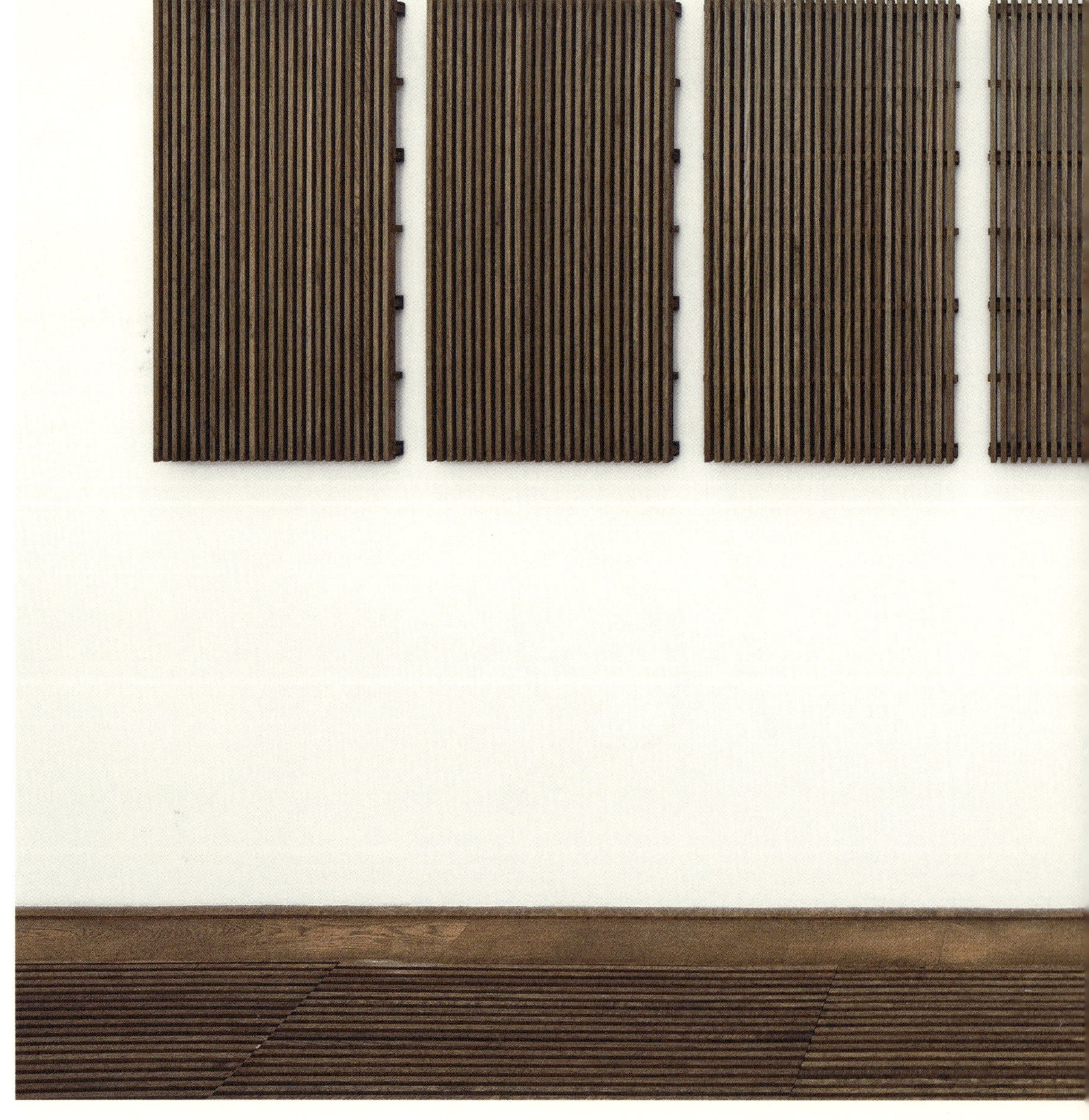

14   *Week*, Kunsthalle Basel, 2012

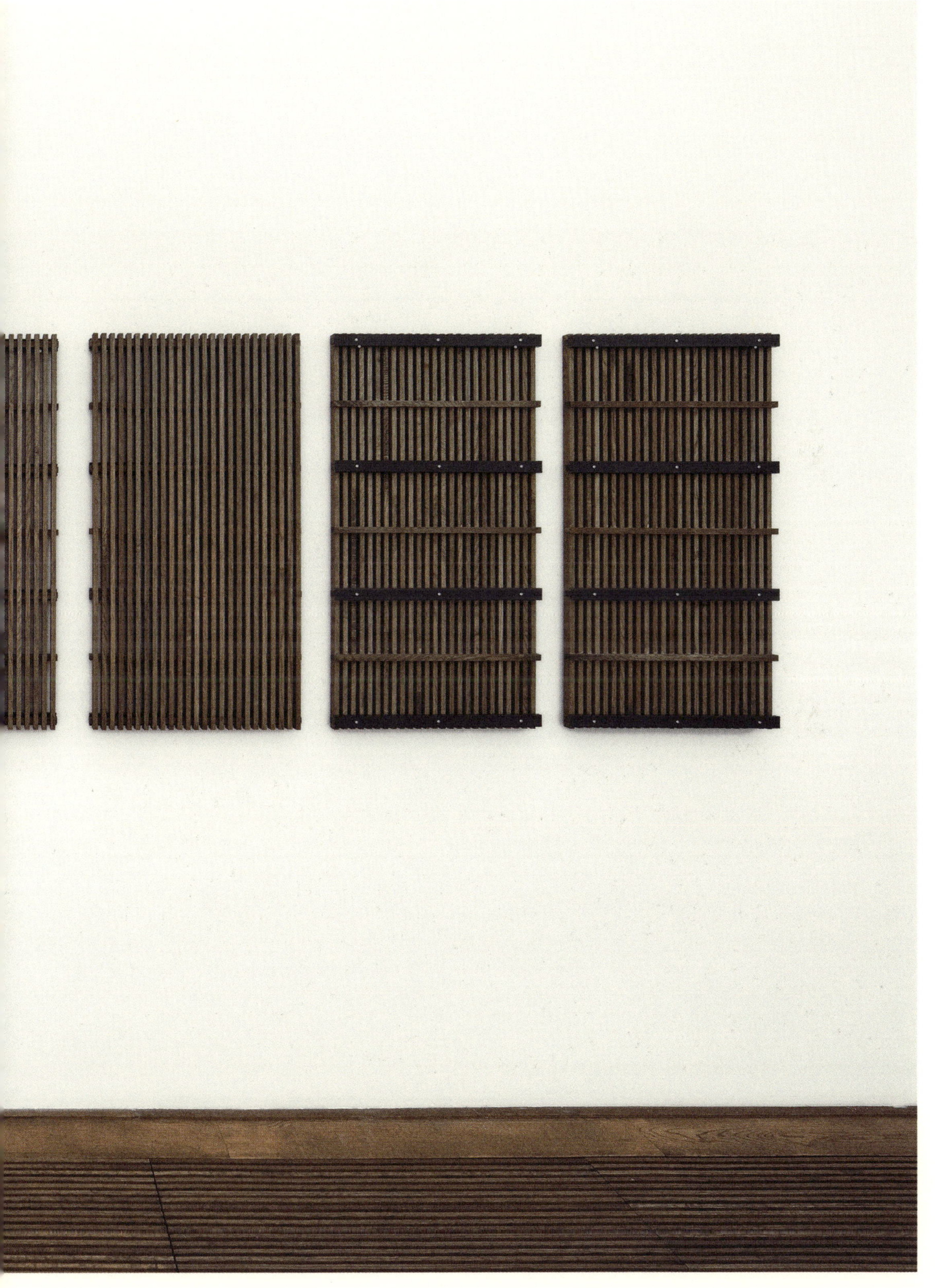

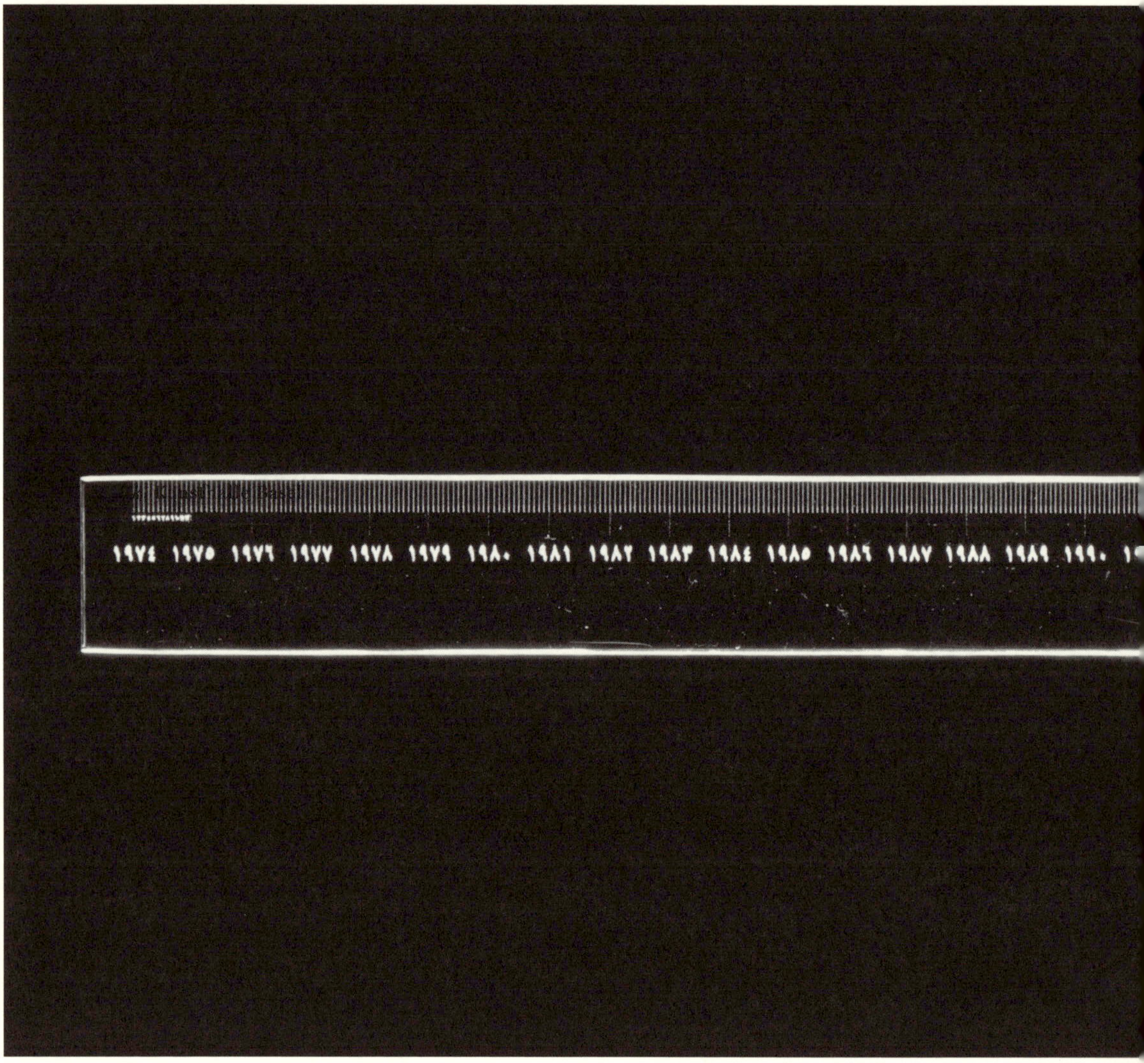

Ruler I (Cairo), 2007

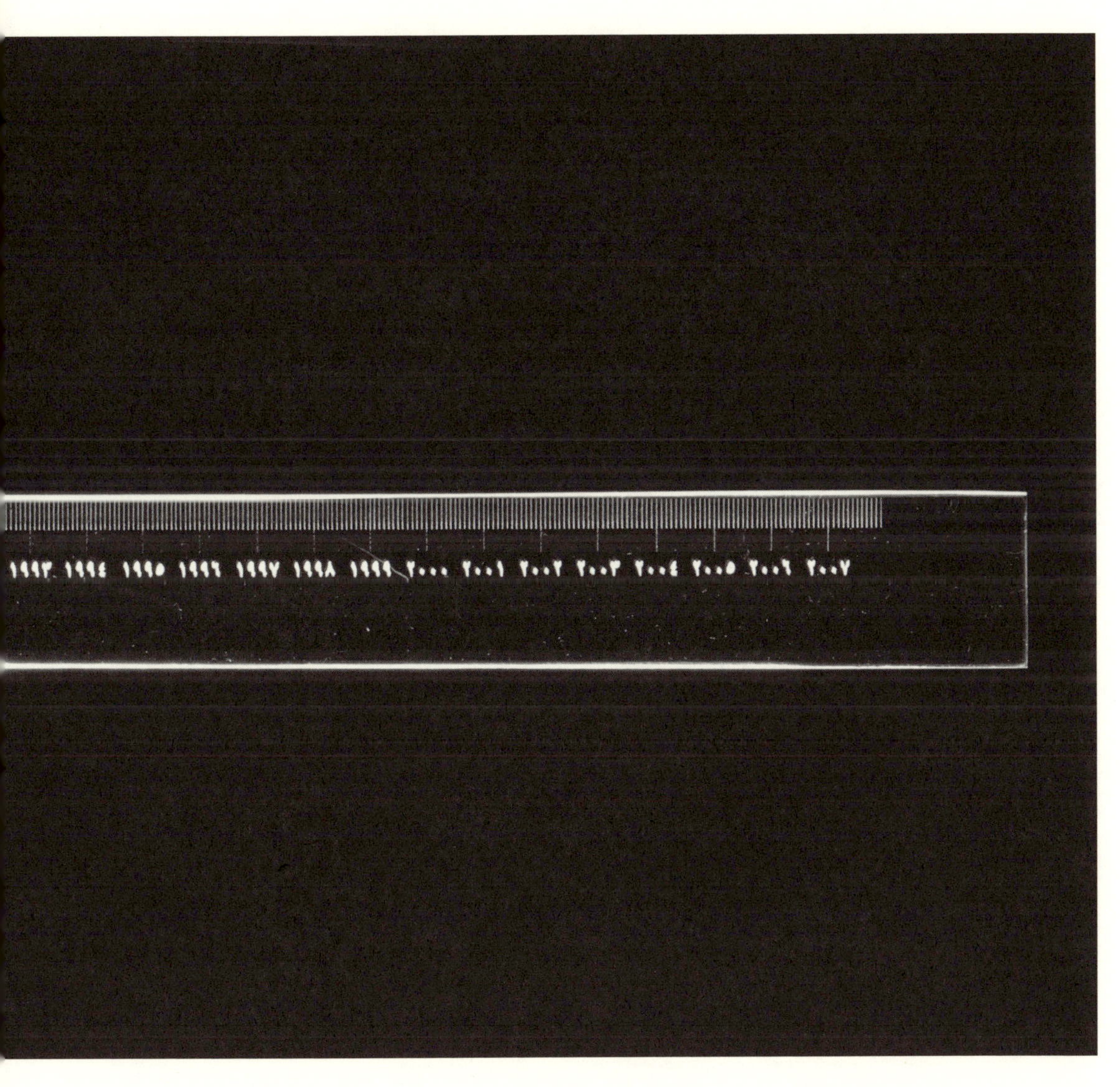

١٩٩٣ ١٩٩٤ ١٩٩٥ ١٩٩٦ ١٩٩٧ ١٩٩٨ ١٩٩٩ ٢٠٠٠ ٢٠٠١ ٢٠٠٢ ٢٠٠٣ ٢٠٠٤ ٢٠٠٥ ٢٠٠٦ ٢٠٠٧

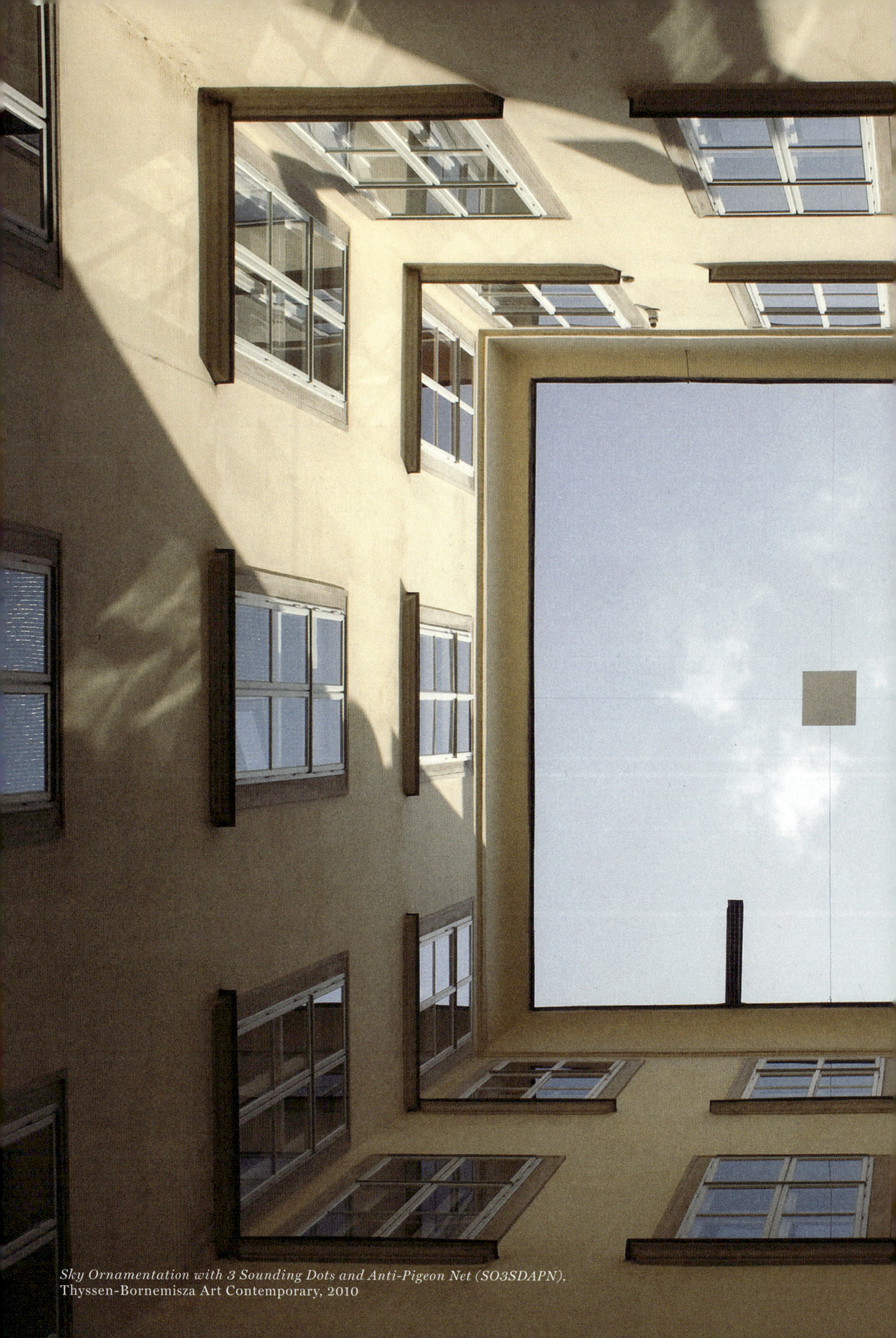

Sky Ornamentation with 3 Sounding Dots and Anti-Pigeon Net (SO3SDAPN),
Thyssen-Bornemisza Art Contemporary, 2010

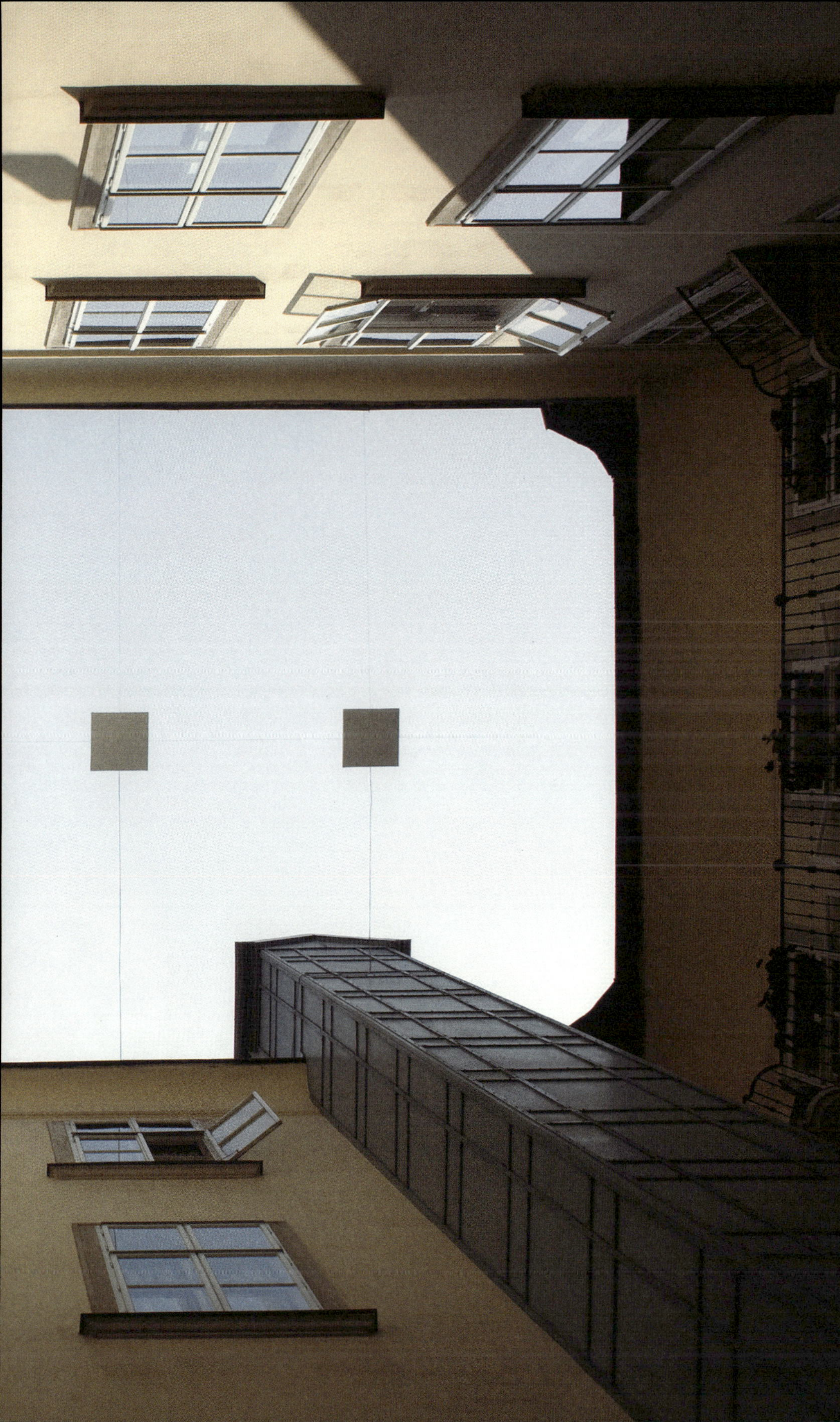

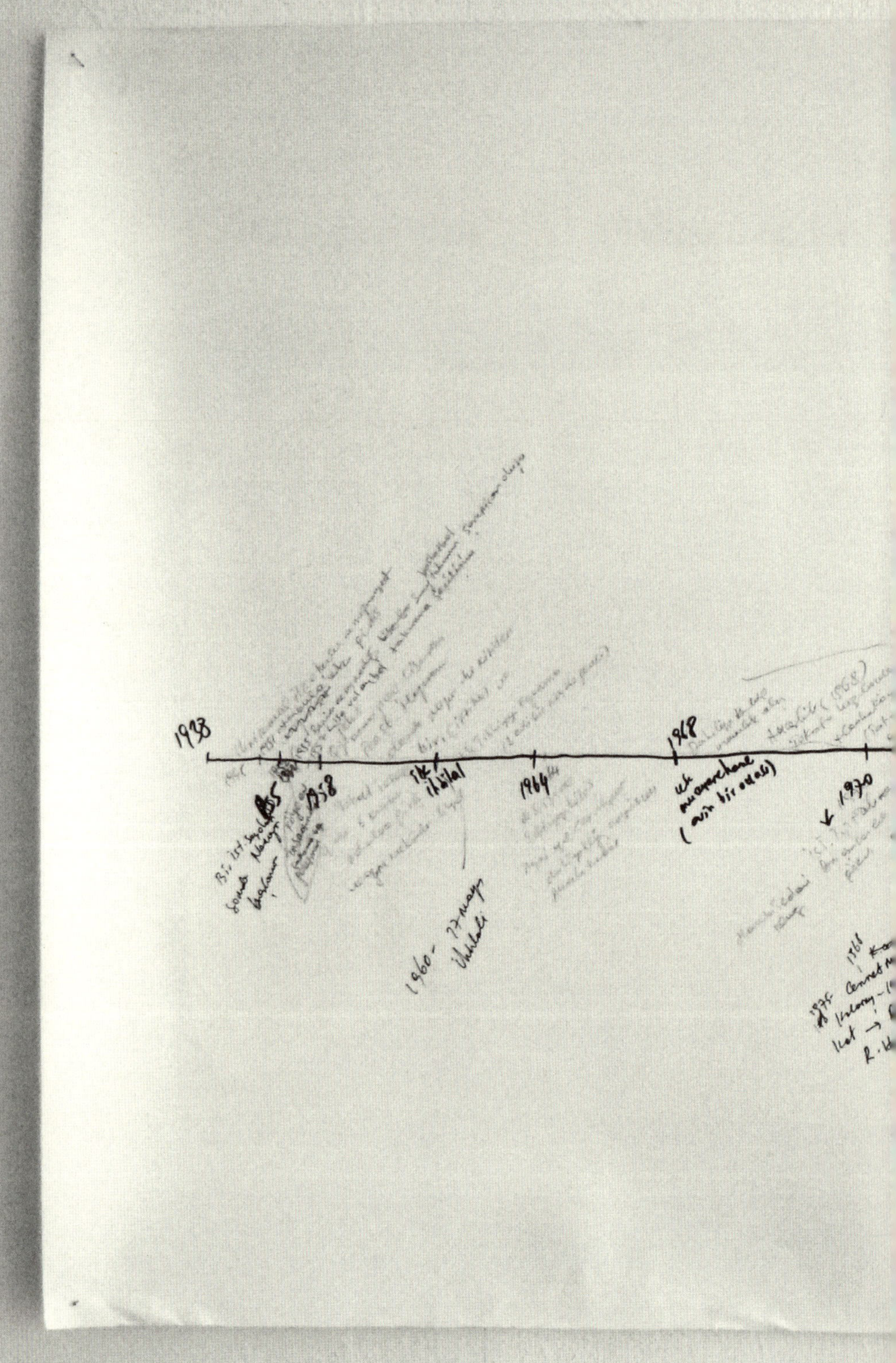

Father's Timeline, 2007

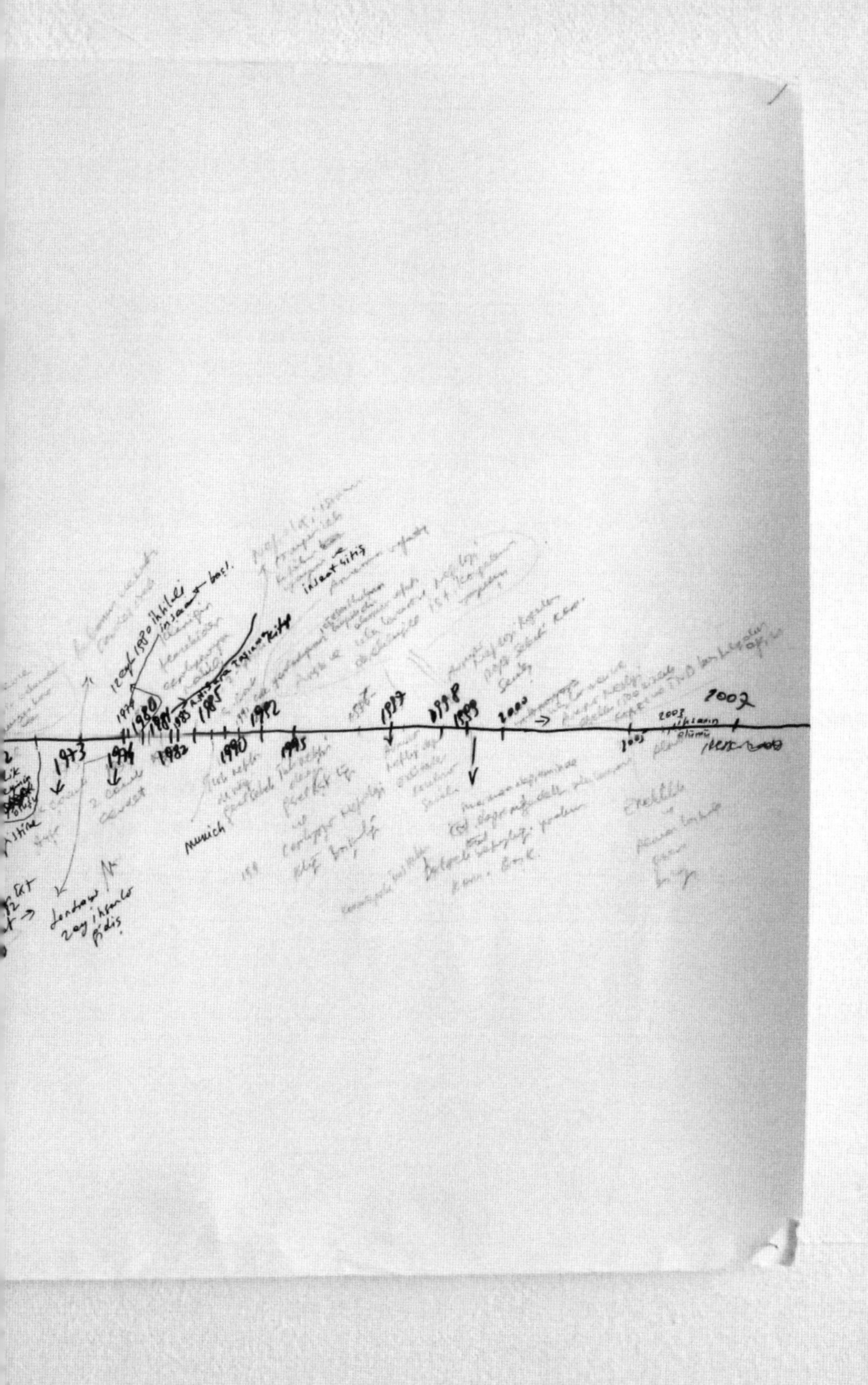

1973
1976
1980
1982
1990
1995
1997
1998
1999
2000
2002
2003

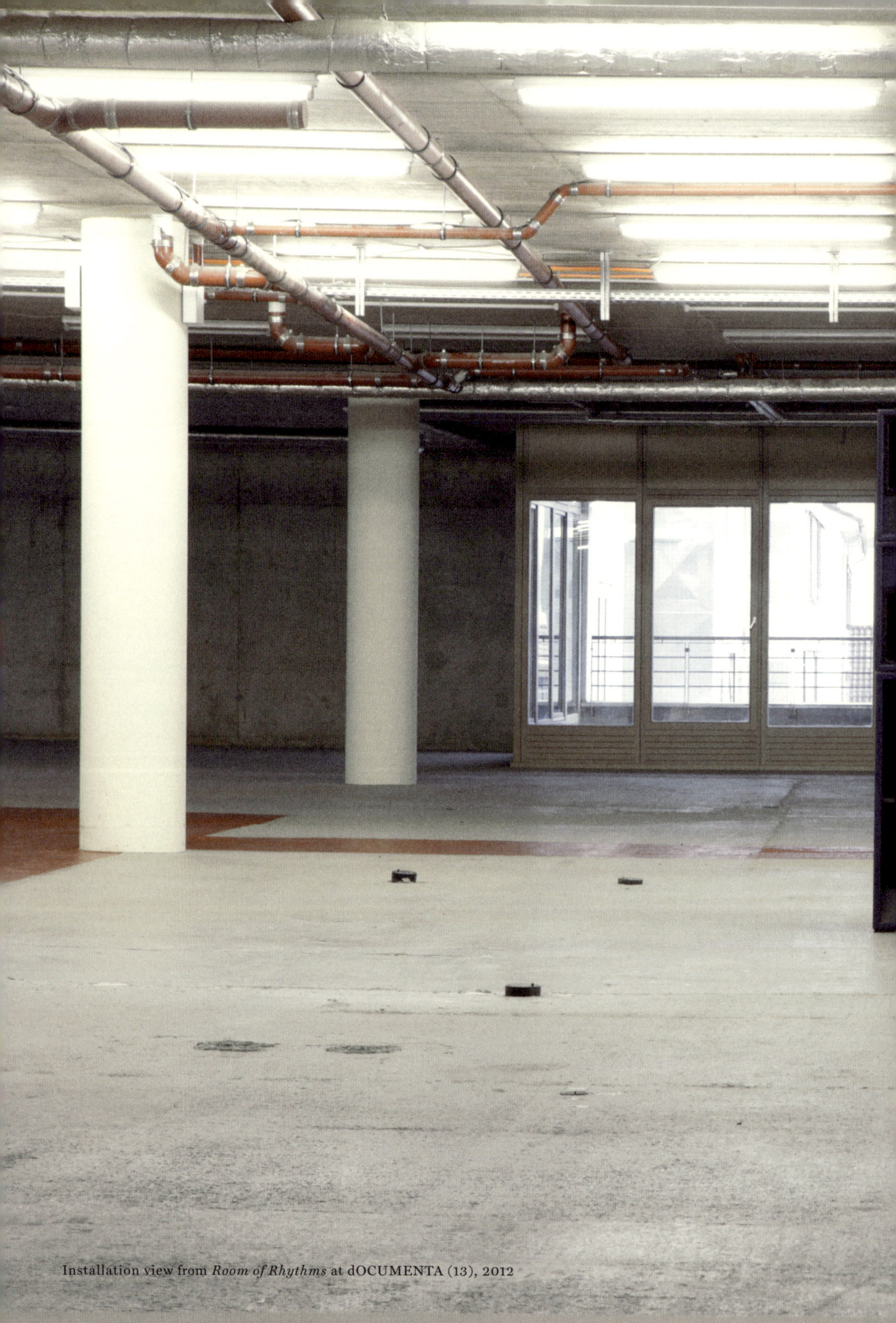

Installation view from *Room of Rhythms* at dOCUMENTA (13), 2012

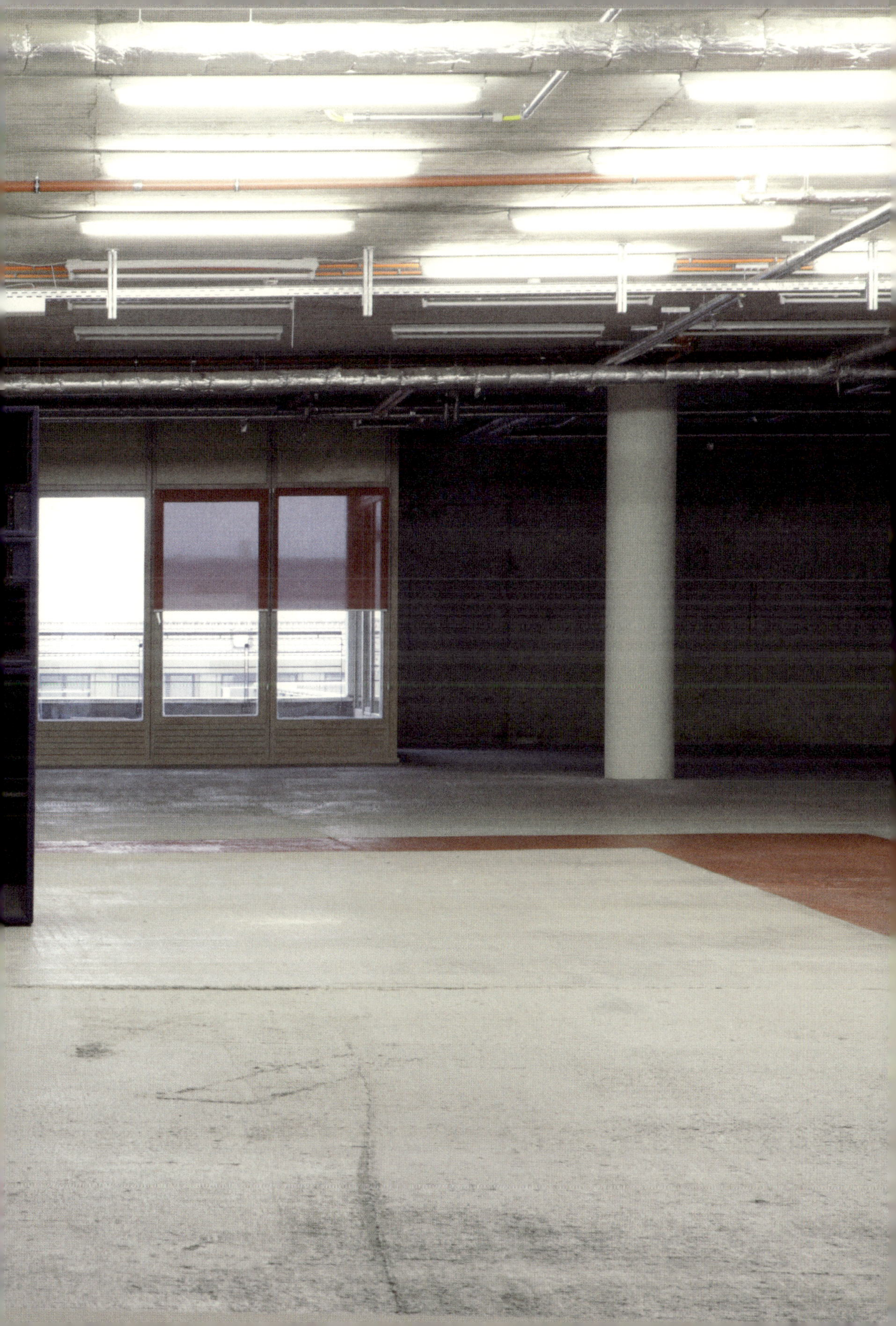

<table>
<tr><td>

dark

1

breakfast

on

</td><td>

light

0

break fast

off

</td></tr>
</table>

dark   light

1   0

breakfast   break fast

on   off

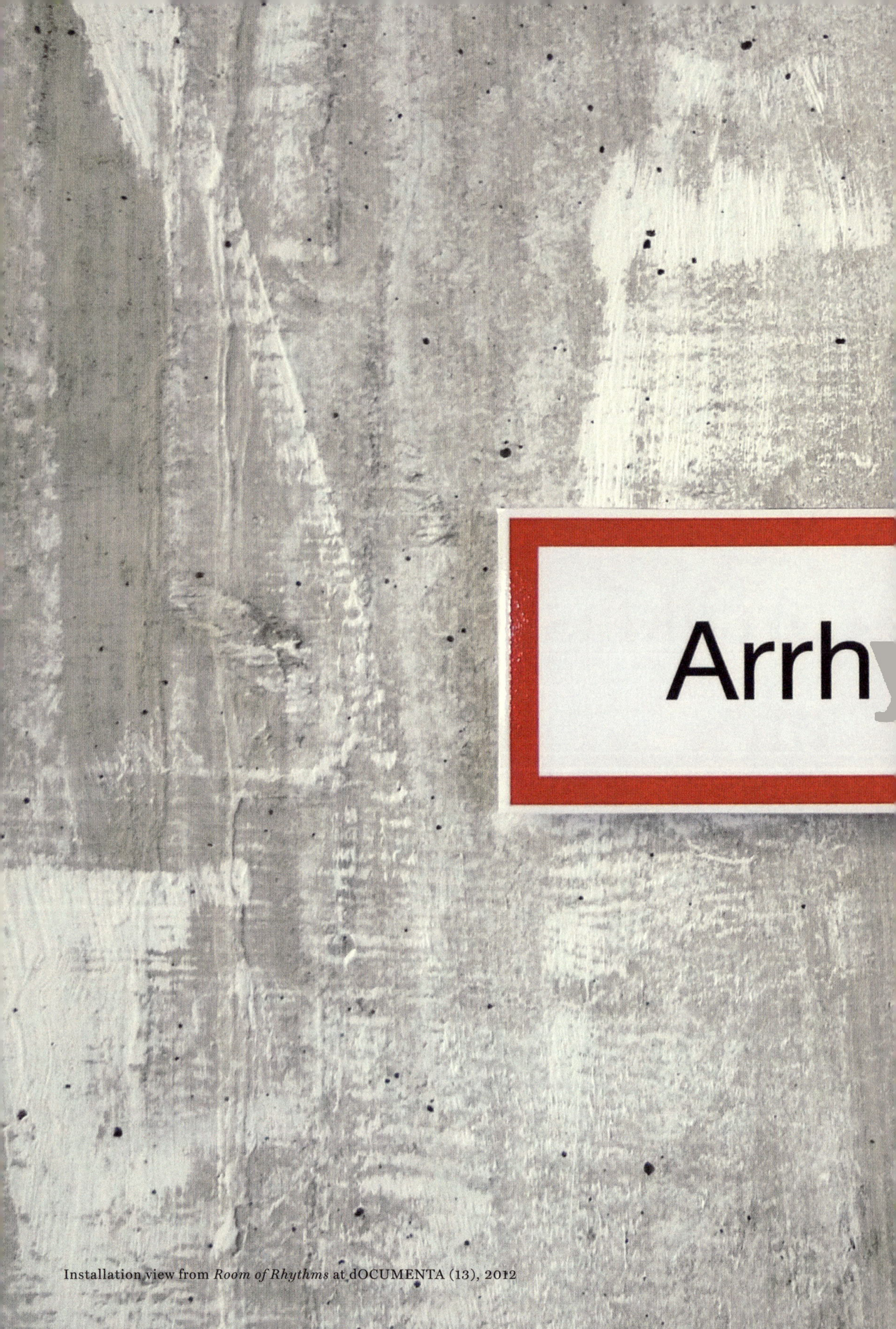

Installation view from *Room of Rhythms* at dOCUMENTA (13), 2012

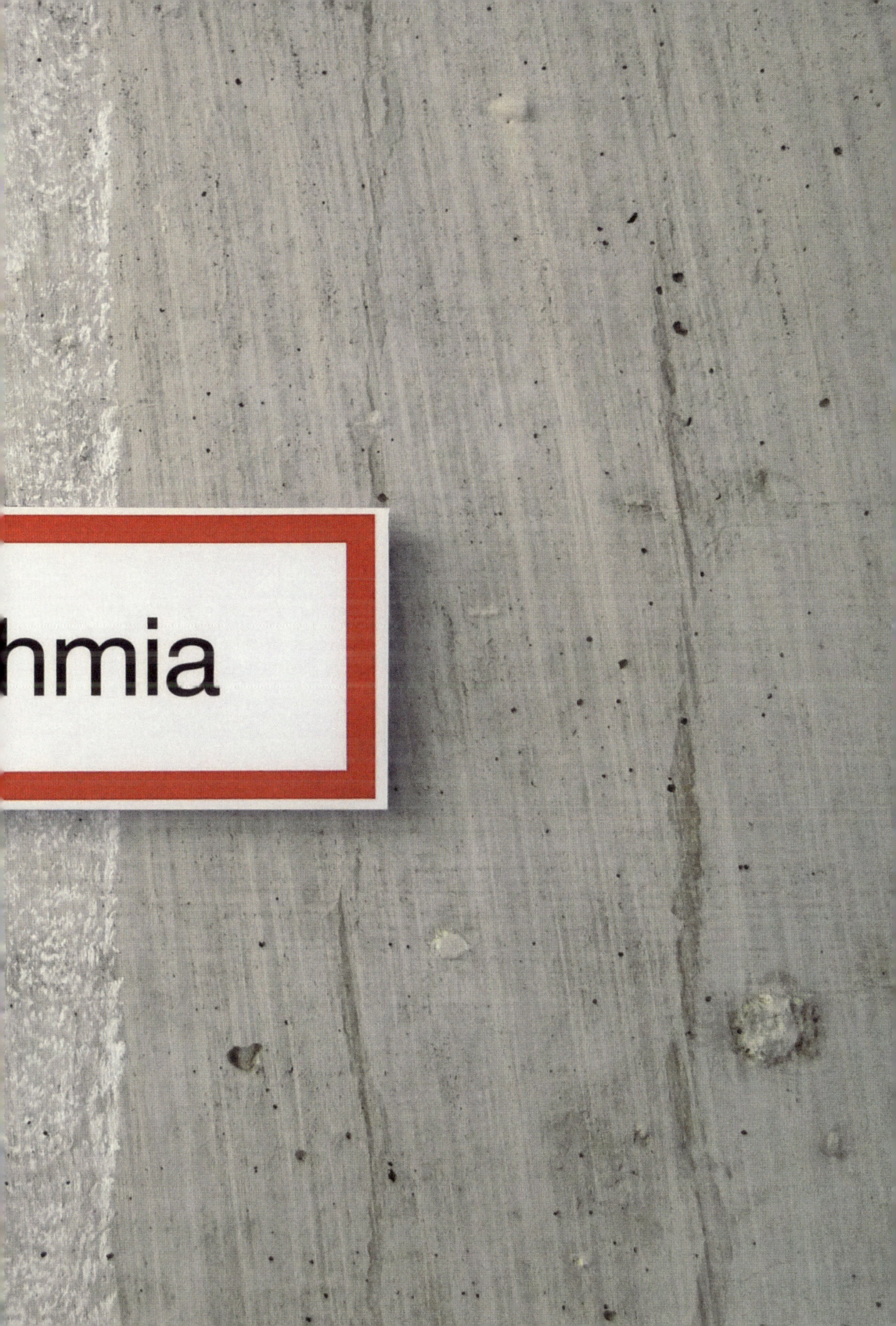

hmia

   Ruler 0 - Now, 2007

now

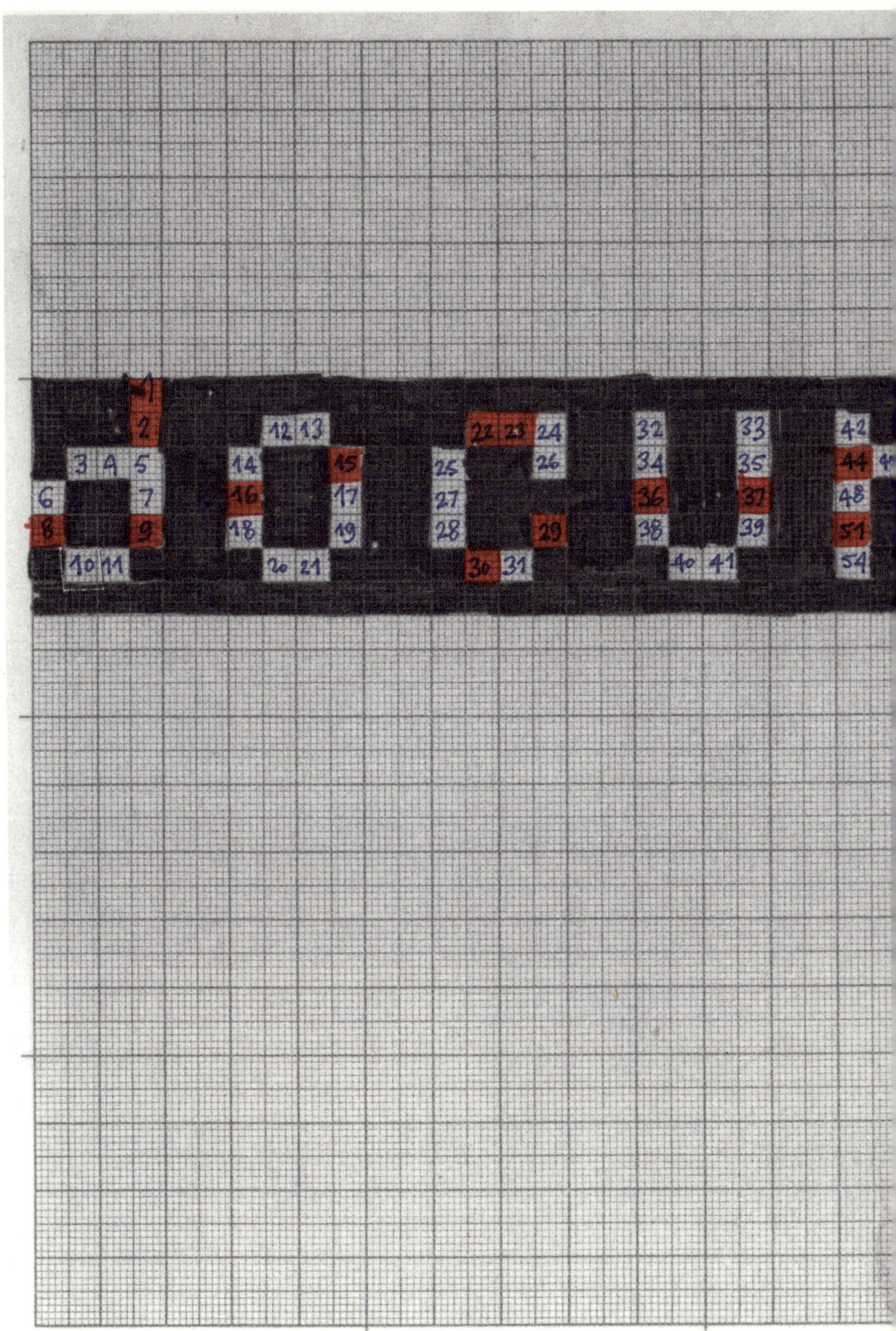

30   Sketch for *Time Chart for the Documenta Worker*, 2012 (Red squares indicate weekends.
Letters are based on Lo-Res, a bitmap font family designed by Zuzana Licko, 1985 and 2011.)

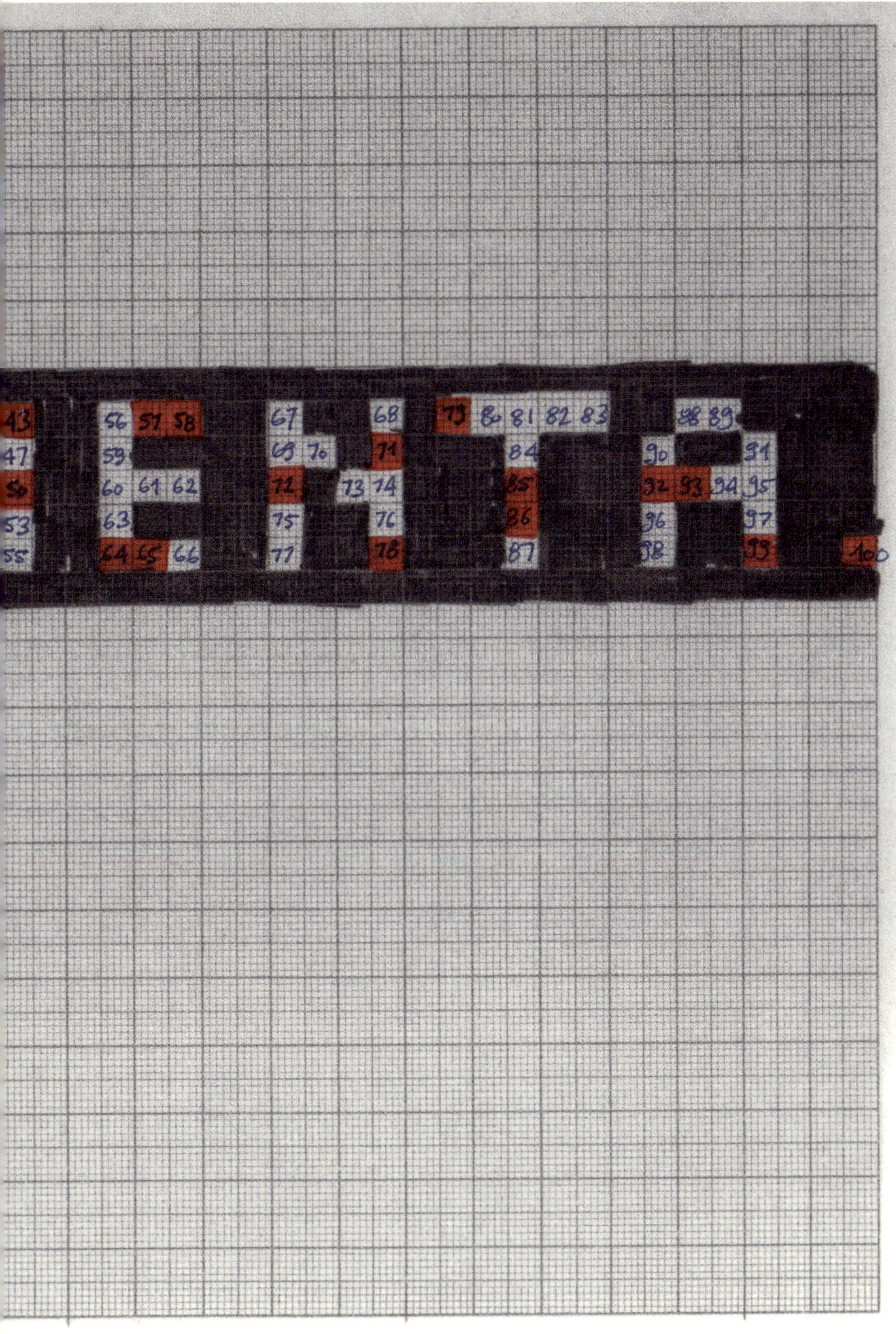

43
47
50
53
55
56 57 58
59
60 61 62
63
64 65 66
67
69 70
72
75
77
68
71
73 74
76
78
79 80 81 82 83
84
85
86
87
88 89
90
92 93 94 95
96
98
91
97
99
100

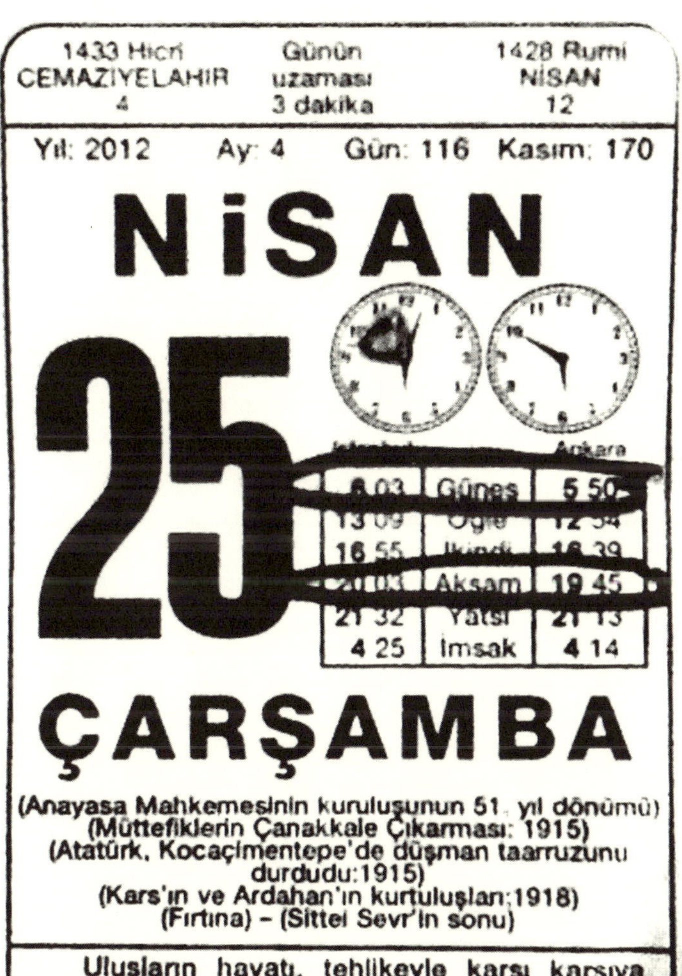

1433 Hicri
CEMAZIYELAHIR
4
Günün
uzaması
3 dakika
1428 Rumi
NİSAN
12
Yıl: 2012   Ay: 4   Gün: 116   Kasım: 170
NİSAN
25
İstanbul
Ankara
6 03 | Güneş | 5 50
13 09 | Öğle | 12 54
16 55 | İkindi | 16 39
| Aksam | 19 45
21 32 | Yatsı | 21 13
4 25 | İmsak | 4 14
ÇARŞAMBA
(Anayasa Mahkemesinin kuruluşunun 51. yıl dönümü)
(Müttefiklerin Çanakkale Çıkarması: 1915)
(Atatürk, Kocaçimentepe'de düşman taarruzunu
durdudu:1915)
(Kars'ın ve Ardahan'ın kurtuluşları:1918)
(Fırtına) – (Sittei Sevr'in sonu)
Ulusların hayatı, tehlikeyle karşı karşıya
kalmadıkça, savaş cinayettir. – Atatürk
Saatli Maarif Takvimi

A Conversation

Duygu Demir: Cevdet, could *Room of Rhythms*, created in Kassel for dOCUMENTA (13), be described as the culmination and the final statement in a series of experiments you have been conducting through your work, the start of which can be traced back to *1/86400*, your earliest work, a video countdown from 2003?

Cevdet Erek: It is not a final statement; I would have really liked it to be, but that doesn't seem possible at the moment or ever really. In *Room of Rhythms* — let's call it *RoR* from now on — I am able to propose something that wasn't possible in other experimentations I had been doing on different occasions. With *RoR*, for the first time, I am free to define a larger space (even though, as a former C&A children's department store, it is not a space designed for exhibitions) through the use of sounds accompanied by architectural and graphic gestures. On the other hand, it is not fully resolved; the work does not totally take control of the environment.

RoR employs the vocabulary and structure of minimal dance music, and refers to the spaces where such sounds are used communally; which could be either a club or a temporary venue for techno parties. *Week,* which was a similar but smaller-scale installation at Kunsthalle Basel in 2011, was a trial run for this; there, the sound piece (the beat) was formed by and limited to the temporal unit of a week, and its subdivision, a day. In *RoR*, there are other temporal units, such as the periodicity and duration of Documenta itself, which is once every five years for one hundred days. Also, the architecture of the space plays a more vital role. The project at Kunsthalle Basel ignored the architecture in a way; it partially blocked it rather than pointing to it or replicating it. At Documenta, I am appropriating the architectural language, whereas in the main space at Kunsthalle Basel, the architecture mostly acted as a container for artificial sound and natural light. And in this way, the architecture of the building becomes more apparent as a subject, especially the parts of it that are in sync with the sonic.

DD: Could you elaborate more on how you had a different approach to engaging with the architecture of the space at Kunsthalle Basel? I think you create a dialogue with the building in Basel as well.

CE: The architecture of the building was an important concern, but I was interested in something that had to do with the Oberlicht (skylight). There, the only interaction was with natural light that came from the skylights above. The relationship was established through the denial of the existing acoustic space by proposing a new one. This defines the space right under the skylights by hanging two layers of white fabric over the constructed rectangular aluminum truss system, which also blocked off the existing ornamentation. So, the dialogue was with the light in the space and the void, not with the architecture that enveloped it. At the former C&A store in Kassel, the space and its architecture say something else, like: "look at me," "look out the windows," "walk around." There is quite a lot of daylight here, again, but it is not very dramatic or dominant. There is no ornamentation; instead, the ceiling is covered with elements of ventilation, electrical wiring, etc. The two buildings say very different things, but in terms of engaging with the architecture, I guess the approach is similar: listening to what the space says and responding to it.

When you produce a sound in a space, the space then responds to it acoustically by creating reverberations, etc. Simultaneously, there is another kind of dynamic, which is very similar to the phenomenon of acoustic impulse response. This is between the architecture and the person who engages with it. The space sends an impulse, and the installation or intervention responds to it, and yet another layer is added with the viewers' reaction.

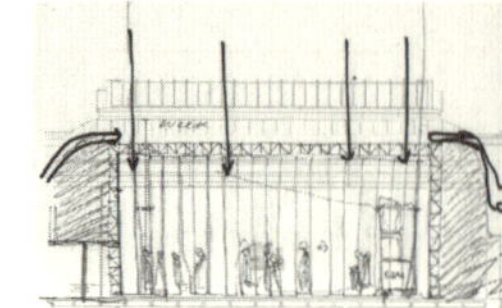

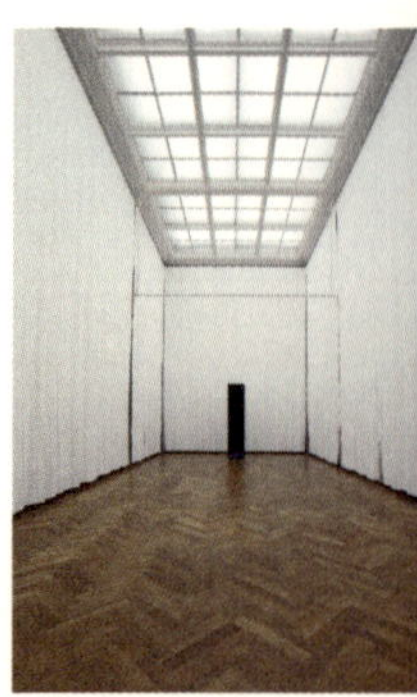

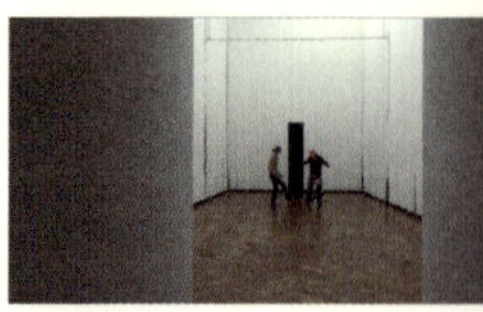

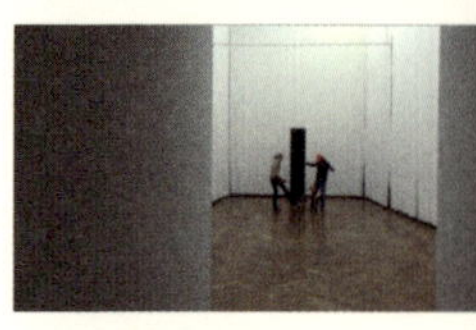

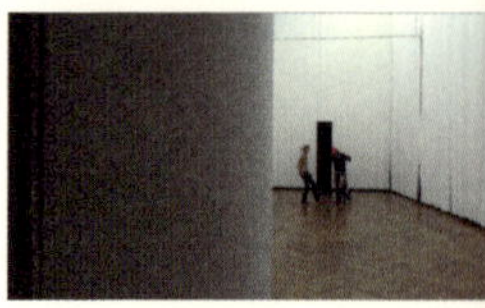

Sketch for and installation images of *Week*, Kunsthalle Basel, 2012 ^
Installation view from *Week*, 2012 ›

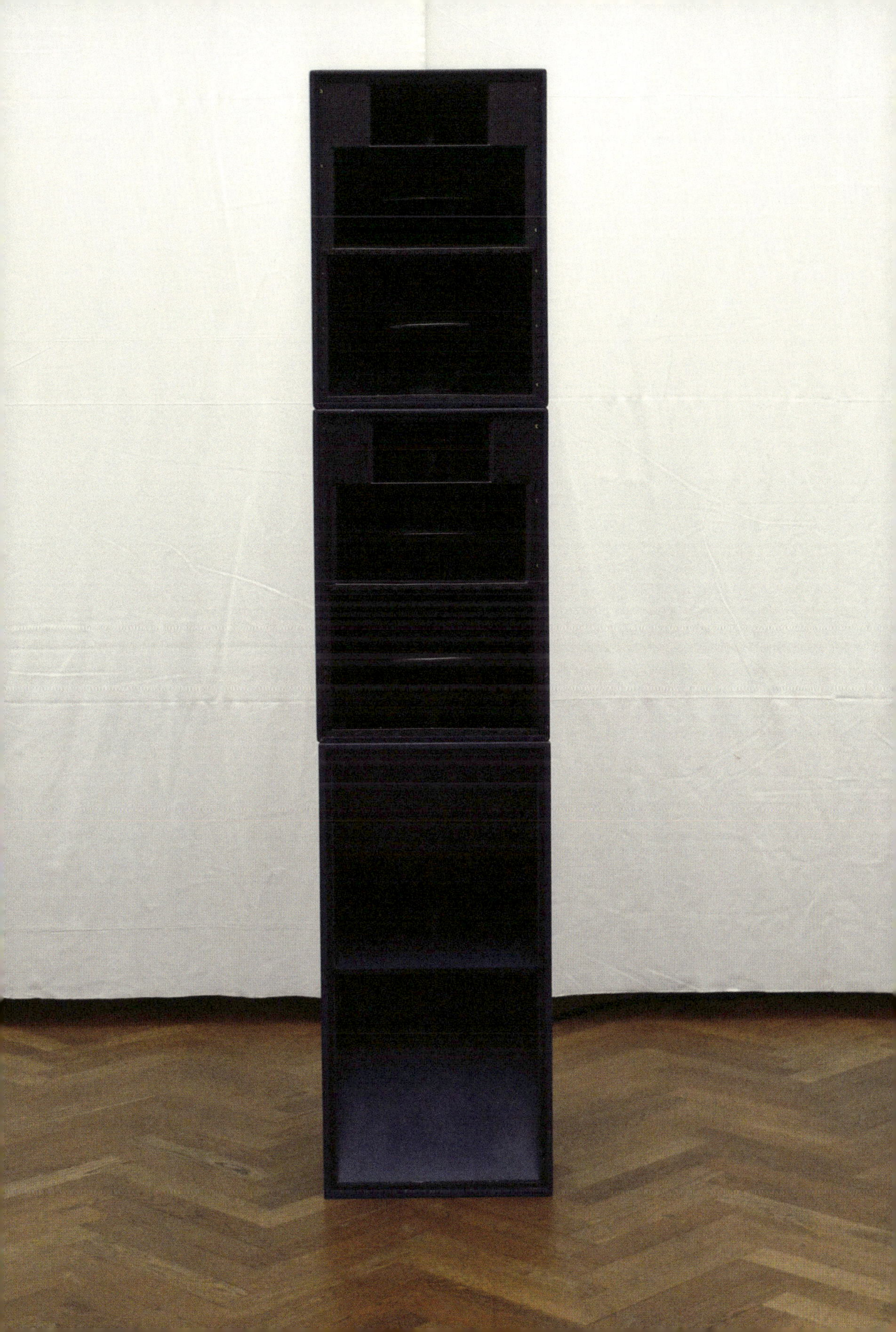

DD: We could say that the three core principles of International Style are "ornament is a crime," "truth to materials," and "form follows function." *RoR* will be situated in a building with modernist attributes. What is your relationship with International Style and the idea of modernism in architecture?

CE: Measured time signifies a drive for standardization, and a motivation to divide time into unchanging units that can be safely used by everyone. If we plan to meet at 9 a.m. the worst that can happen is for me to be half an hour late, like I was today. But neither of us has any doubt as to when 9 a.m. is, because the majority of us — those of us who live in synchronicity with the clock or the calendar at least — use the same system to read time. The Internet altered our way of perceiving time and space, but still, a conventional system, based on hours, a.m. and p.m. is widely used. We accept it and are dominated by a standardized notion of time. This reminds me of Peter Weibel's proposition, *chronocracy*. During a train ride to Frankfurt just a few weeks ago, I ran into Peter Weibel and asked him how he would compare International Style to music. We were talking about International Style in architecture and the visual arts. His reply was exactly what I anticipated: "techno." Techno has been almost the same in urban centers around the world for the last thirty-plus years. Dancing to a repetitive beat is not a contemporary act; it is as old as you can imagine, but the fact that techno is produced with a drum machine or with computers, that everybody uses more or less similar samples (bass drum samples from the analogue world), that all of these are downloadable via the Internet, that similar rhythms are played in clubs all around the world, almost always reduced to a single beat, the bpm of which doesn't alternate over time… All of these attributes can be seen within the framework of the three principles you mentioned or the idea of standardization I was talking about. When this so-called mechanized organization of sounds — be it techno or minimal house — is played somewhere, it fulfills a ritualistic need and activates people, prompting them to tap or clap and to interact with each other, moving with the beat. (Or similarly, when played in a department store, it prompts people to shop.)

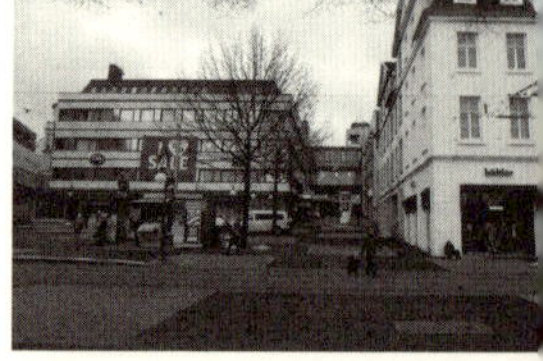

This connection is present in *RoR*. The building that hosts *RoR* is not the flagship building of modernism per se, but it carries some of its typical characteristics in terms of its structure, volume and facade, especially with its large windows.

DD: What are you doing with the windows at the C&A space?

CE: A very simple visualization, it is related to the idea of *Week*, again. In Kassel, what struck my attention in some of the modernist buildings were the window blinds, which we no longer really get to see on the exteriors of buildings in Istanbul. The space that I am working with has two terraces that jut into the interior, and one of these structures coincidentally has windows with seven partitions. I am not at all intentionally looking for specific numbers, but the entrance axis of the space points to these seven partitions. So I am placing two blinds in the last two partitions on the right. It is a rather banal graphic visualization, referencing the week and the weekend. And in front of them is a loudspeaker, playing the sonification of a week, just like in Basel. Behind them is an anti-pigeon net, pixelating the view outside.

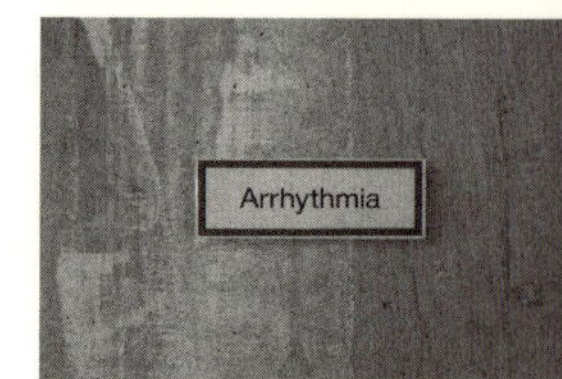

DD: And in this way, you are employing words from a vocabulary of materials and concerns that you have created over time.

CE: Exactly. This is not a novel idea but what interested me was using two-dimensional elements made for a three-dimensional space, as in graphic illustration. At the same time, the blinds signify the weekend. The two windows at the end are closed, limiting the daylight.

Exterior of C&A building in Kassel, *Room of Rhythms*, 2012 ˄
Installation view from *Room of Rhythms* at dOCUMENTA (13), 2012 ˃

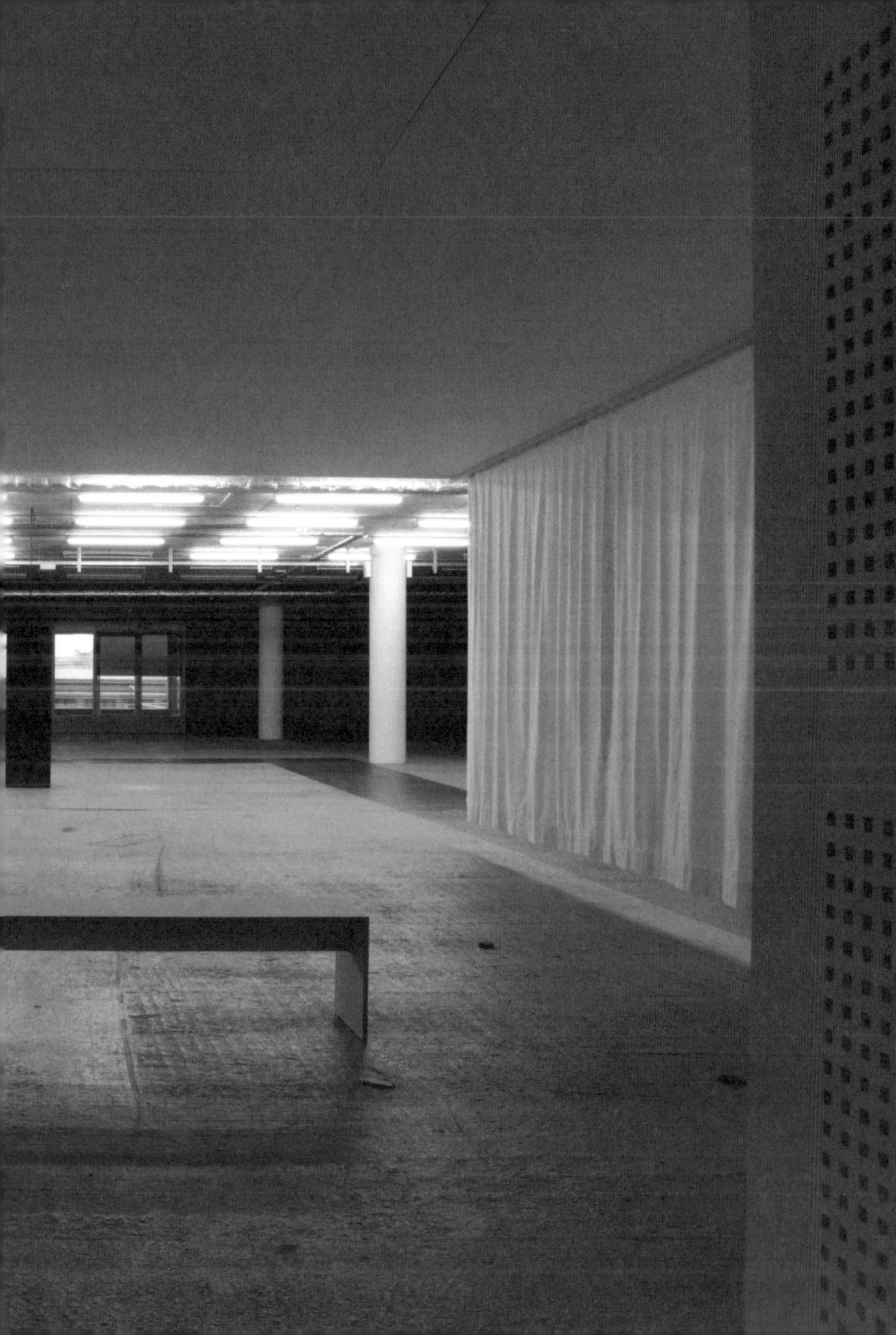

DD: As if to say, "it is the weekend, and we are closed."

CE: I guess it could be read in that way. I am looking for simple and pre-existing elements to construct a stage for making potential connections.

DD: When you were talking about these windowpanes, you also mentioned a column. You sometimes also activate columns through sound.

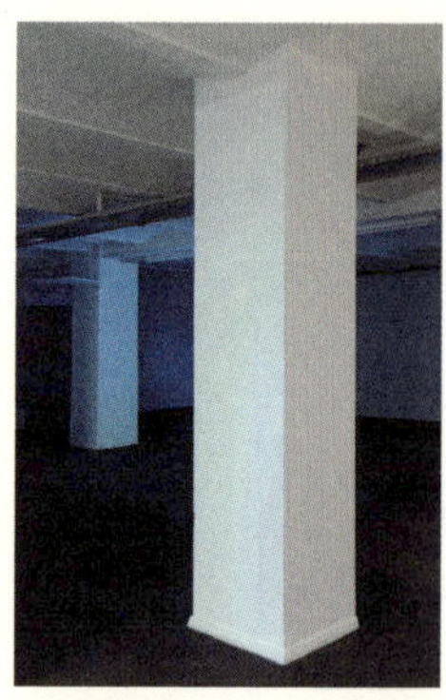

CE: Yes, that's true. But in Kassel, it is not a literal structural element, but a column comprised of loudspeakers. I think you are making a connection with a previous work, *Kolon*. In Turkish *kolon* refers to a column as an architectural element as well as to loudspeakers that amplify sound. I made the work *Kolon* for a rather crowded touring group exhibition. The exhibition space, Tanas in Berlin, was fully occupied. The intention was to make a site-specific work, but I had to come up with something almost invisible so that it didn't block the view of the other works in the exhibi-tion — bear in mind that the title of the exhibition was *Tactics of Invisibility*. I inserted an extra column in the extant grid of columns in the space, in which I placed loudspeakers that played a multiplied sampled sound taken from the beeping of traffic lights. A traffic light beeper borrowed from the city of Kassel is also used in *RoR*. The beep, or more precisely the *ticking*, is normally used to help the visually impaired cross the street. It is similar to the mirroring of the window panel pattern within the space in *RoR*, because of the insertion of additional structures that simul-taneously play on and blend in with the existing architecture.

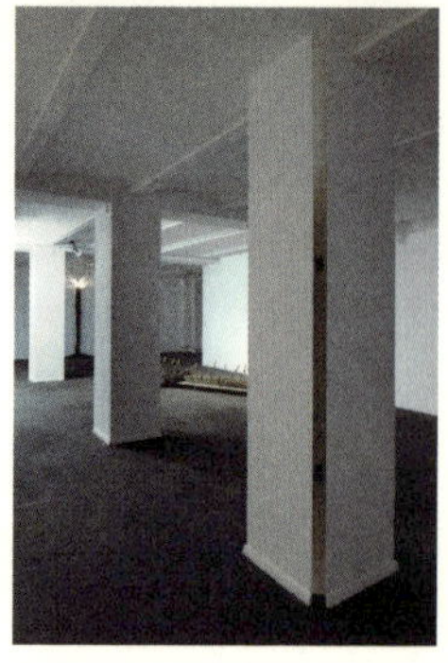

DD: So you are multiplying the pre-existing architectural elements.

CE: In a way, this is also a kind of sampling.

DD: And sampling is also a tactic used in music frequently.

CE: Of course. It is not a tactic, but rather a device.

DD: Then what you did with *Kolon* embodies two kinds of sampling. You take a sound from the street, record it and use it after altering it. At the same time, you are sampling the architecture of the exhibition space by taking a pre-existing element and duplicating it.

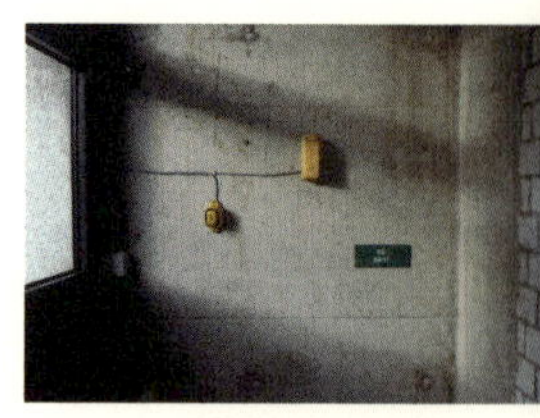

CE: Yes, altering or obliterating its function, and using it again. The column was no longer a support structure; it was a copy. Visually, it still performs the same func-tion; it is a column in the space, in the background, just like the others, almost un-noticeable.

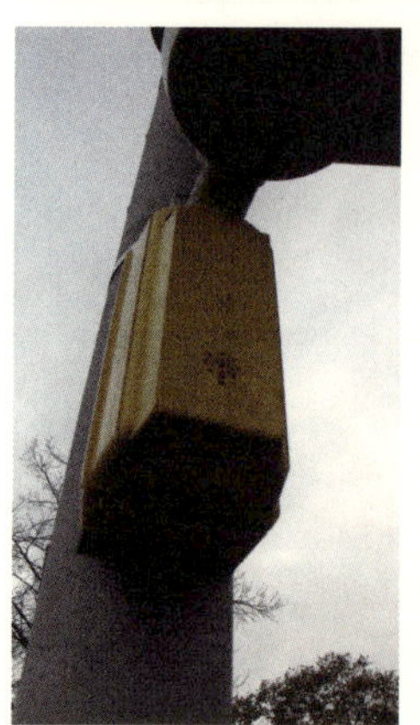

The sound at the traffic light was like this: tak-tak-tak-tak... One beat per second. When the light turned green for pedestrians, it turned into something else: dit-dit-dit-dit-dit... In the exhibition space, it becomes a sound that draws people in or tells them to stop there briefly. The processed sound samples constructed a new pattern and it was harder to dissect; a cloud made up of dots. So yes, these are two kinds of sampling.

DD: When you were talking about modernist architecture and International Style, you talked about standardization, of things being the same all over the world. There is a common and easily recognizable language. You also said that in music, this no-tion of standardization is embodied in techno. Can we consider this idea of stand-ardization in relation to your *Ruler* series?

CE: Absolutely.

Installation views from *Kolon* at Tanas, 2010 ʌ
Installation view from *Kolon* at Arter, 2011 ›

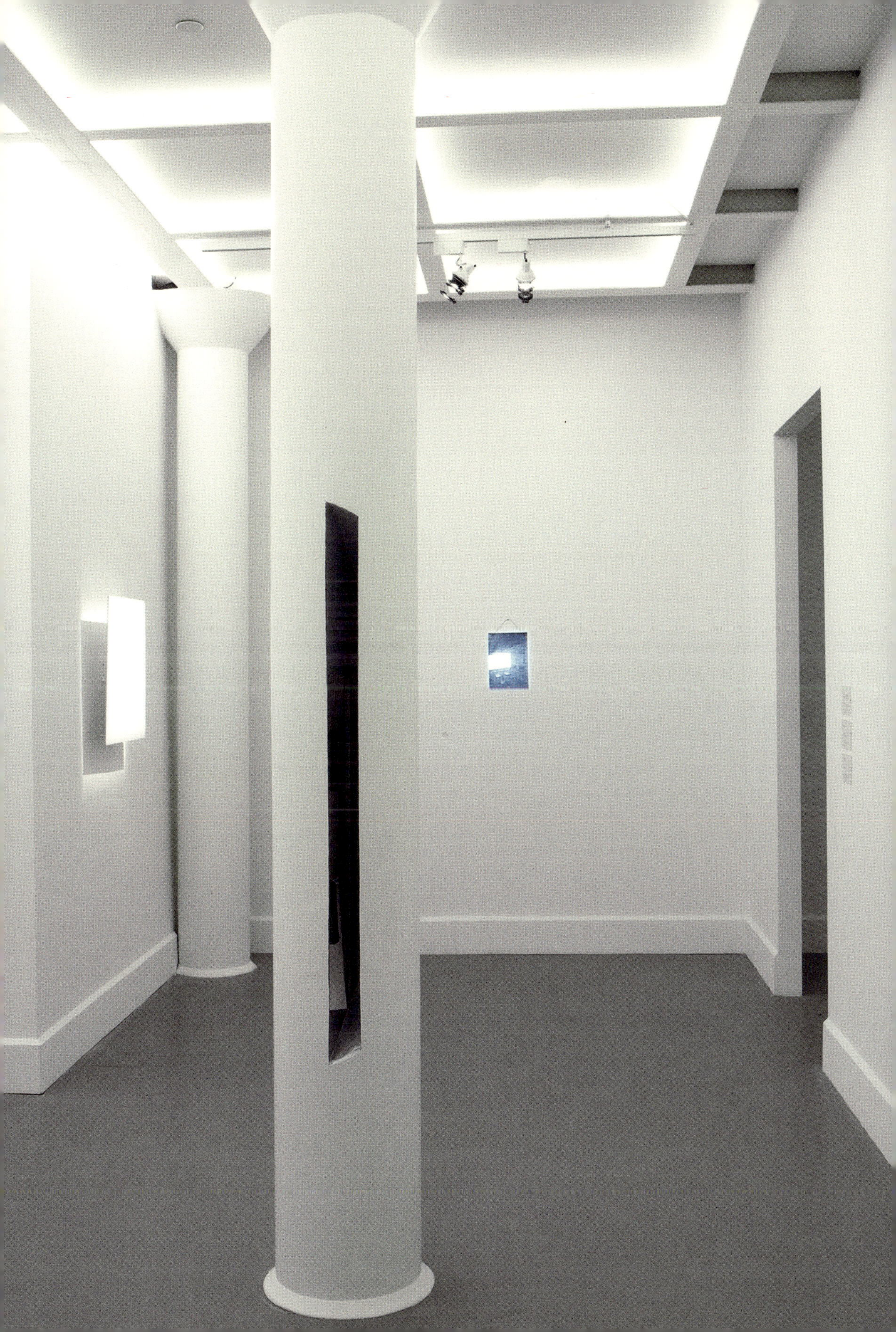

DD: What was the first ruler that you made?

CE: When I chat with people, I scribble things; make drawings or simple time-lines on pieces of paper. This was before I had made any rulers; I wasn't even using any with which to draw timelines. The first timeline came about when I was talking to my father, which then became *Father's Timeline*. I drew a line, and told him "you were born here," and that this was the beginning, and towards the end of the line there was a point that indicated 2007 or "the present moment." Then I asked a few questions, such as "When did you move to Istanbul?" or "When did you get married?" These kinds of dates are never forgotten. My father filled in the rest with things that came to his mind within the next five to ten minutes. Did it convey a full picture of my father's life? No. But it captured something that was somewhat linked to reality, or rather something that related to the reality that exists within memory. It is a very simple language. It is not the language of how we live or how we remember things, but we use it; it is practical. After doing this interview with my father, I used this method with other people. Coming back to your question, the first ruler I used during these conversations was a very modest, wooden ruler, thirty centimeters long. During an event called *Black Market for Useful Knowledge and Non-Knowledge* in Istanbul, it occurred to me to use a ruler in order to set a scale that I would use in different drawings. During this time we reduced one year to one cm.

(Reduction is important. When I went to see the site for *RoR*, I noticed the leftover "reduction" [i.e. sale] signs, from the retail store C&A that was there before.

DD: Are you using those?

CE: Yes, the installation team kept some for me; they will be part of *RoR*.)

Some time after these trials I went to Cairo to do a short-term project, and it was Ramadan. The idea of time was very present and dominant because a lot of people had re-adjusted their lives to Ramadan. The life of the city had changed. Meanwhile I was looking for a ruler with Arabic numbers, and couldn't get a hold of one. On the same trip, I also saw very different measurement units of Ancient Egyptians in the museum in Cairo. They are incredible, very small. Then I thought it was a good idea to make a timeline ruler so I could carry it with me, and I wouldn't need to scale one cm to one year each time. We went to a sign maker, and he told us that he would be able to digitally print on something about thirty cm long. I thought about the time span of something that would be roughly thirty years and decided to make a ruler based on my own life span. I put down my birth date, and I stuck to the "one year equals 1 cm" principle from previous interviews. I made a timeline that started with my birth date and ended at the present. This became the first ruler in the series. It was in Arabic, but was read from left to right, because my conception of time then was from left to right. There was also another detail that I forgot to mention; one cm was split into twelve small sections. This was a ruler of measured time, and to indicate time in more detail, we divided the centimeter in the way we divide a year, into twelve months.

DD: When talking about *Father's Timeline*, you mentioned that you can translate this data in the form of a ruler, or you could translate into a sound pattern.

CE: Here is the whole formula — and it applies to *RoR* as well: We make a graphic illustration, which can be translated into sound. This sound uses the vocabulary of dance music. You perceive these sounds with your ear. But they exist within a space. So when you are moving around the space there is an acoustic change.

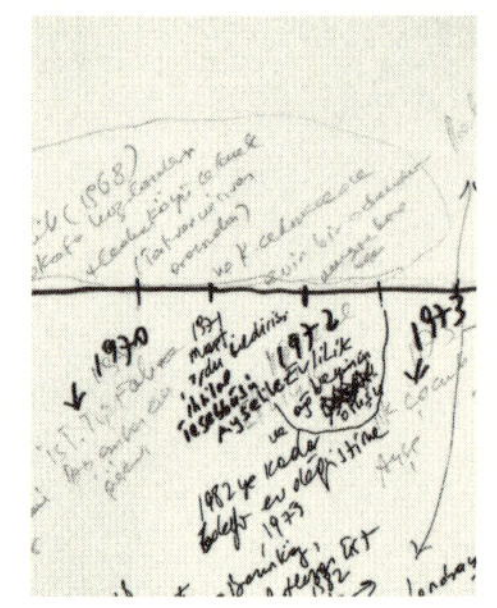

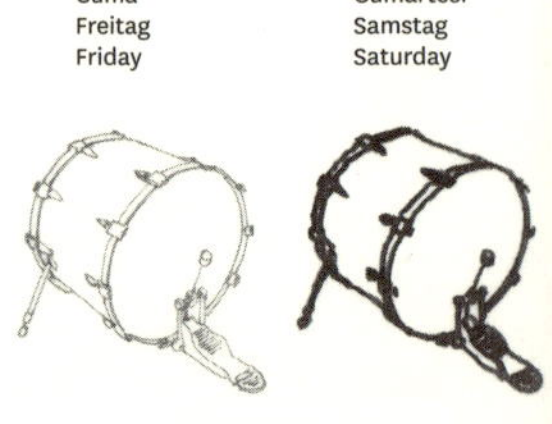

Ruler 1 (Cairo), 2007; *Ruler 1 (Istanbul)*, 2007; *Ruler 1 (Antwerp)* 2009
Installation view from *Rulers and Rhythm Studies*, at *Untitled (12th Istanbul Biennial)*, 2011 >

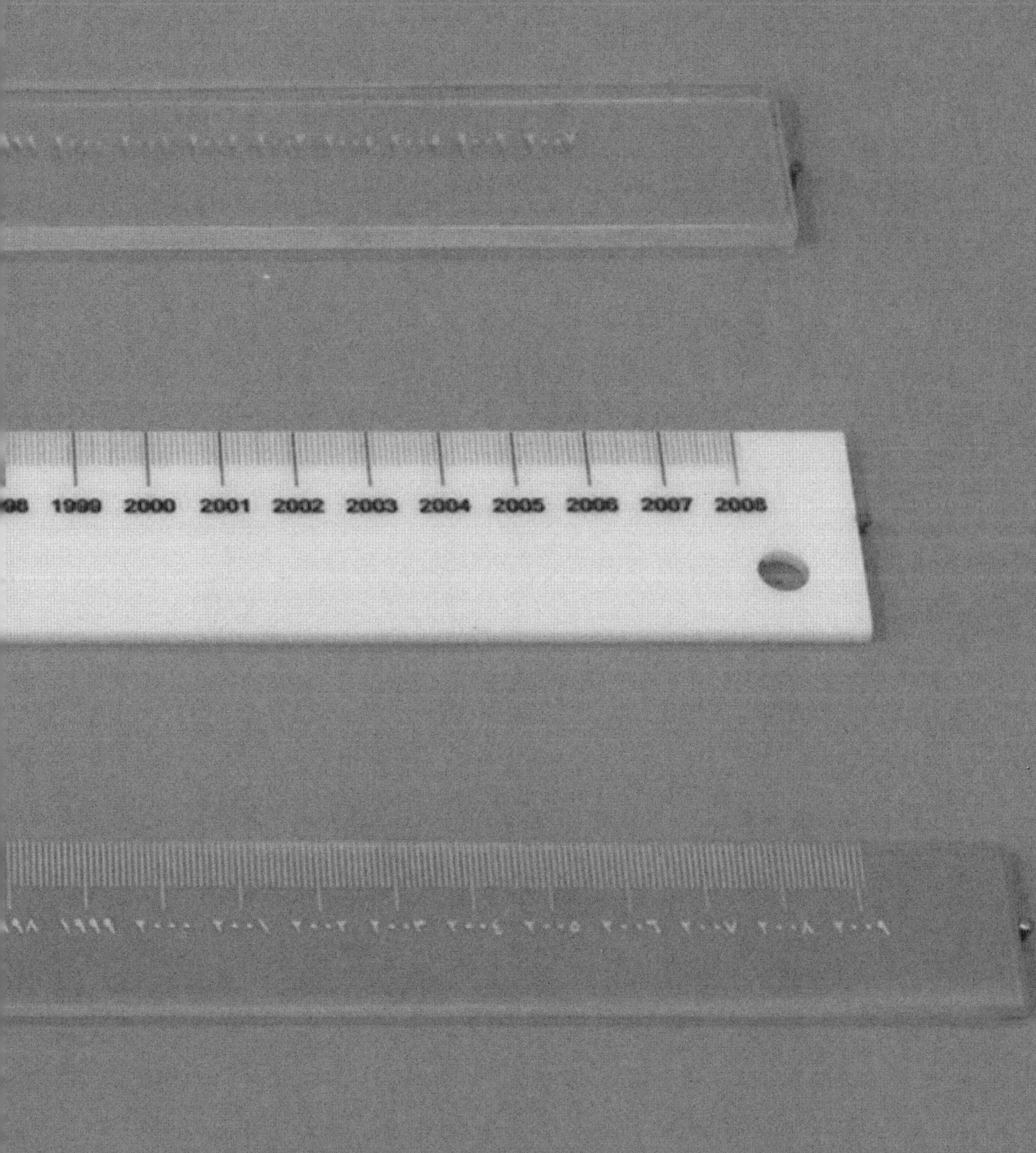

Hopefully, because this is a beat, as you are moving around, this may further translate into dance. The idea of movement is already introduced, if you are part of a group of people, it becomes an event. The name of the performance I did at Kunsthalle Basel was *Several Species of Museum Audience, Gathered Together and Grooving with a Week*. This was done on the Museum Night. The same beat from this performance is also included in *RoR*.

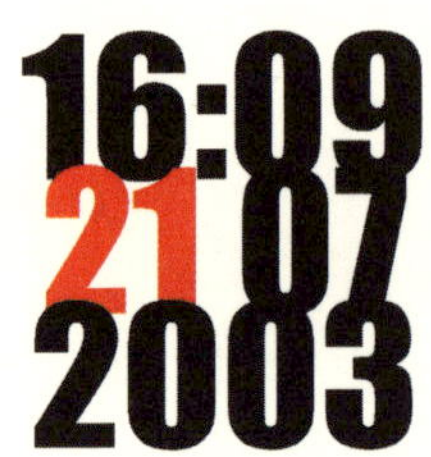

I attempted to do this before, in two earlier works, one of which is *1/86400,* and the other one is *Studio* (2005). In *1/86400,* I used the interface of a calendar, in its simplest form. It was a countdown from when I was commissioned to make this work to when it was shown. It was to be shown only once, during the celebration ceremony of the 230th anniversary of ITU (Istanbul Technical University) — note the culture of the anniversary here. I scaled one second to equal one day, which I have been using for years now, and used simple sounds to mark the beginning, middle and the end of the days. There were additional beats on top of this, some beats for their own sake, so it was more musical, not diagrammatic. But this is the origin of the idea. It was shown in the dark, on a movie screen, and again, night was represented by complete darkness. The weekend was indicated in red numbers.

DD: *Studio* is also an experiment in sonic timelines, isn't it?

CE: Yes. *Father's Timeline* was a drawing, an irregular graphic illustration. *Studio* is based on a video in which two hands are trying to imitate this illustration in sound. I programmed some sound patterns based on some events represented by time data, e.g. the changing five prayer times each day, and borrowed some dates from *Father's Timeline*, and I was trying to imitate it with my hands. As you know, my relationship with music is based on beats, patterns, or rhythms. I couldn't do it perfectly, but something impulsive came about, and I recorded it on camera. It is not an accurate sonic timeline, but a recording of an effort while trying to create a sonic timeline. The recording of the video became an installation. The studio next to mine at Rijksakademie was a photography studio, and I installed the video on the infinity screen of the photography studio. The installation could only be seen through a window next door, from my studio. The video existed on a plane that went from being two-dimensional to three-dimensional. A lot of lights were installed, but most of them were not turned on. The video was projected through one of these lights. But the sound came from my studio.

DD: So *Studio* exists in an in-between space, it is not a direct translation of a timeline but an attempt at sonic or rhythmic mapping perhaps. The process of *Father's Timeline*. And how did the rest of the rulers in the series come into being?

CE: The second ruler was *Ruler 0 - now*. After the first one, it felt necessary to move away from the idea of scale and even from the idea of dates. "0" could correspond to anything, and this way, the personal was eliminated. "0" can be the beginning of anything. And it can signify something different each time. As a user, you assign a meaning to it, but at another time, you can assign it something completely different.

DD: Among your works, this is perhaps the one that I think is most aligned with the Dutch conceptualist Stanley Brouwn. For his work *at this moment the distance between stanley brouwn and yourself is x foot* (1996) he placed a rectangular piece of metal that resembles a ruler on a table. There are no marks on this ruler, and only the title hints at the idea of scale and distance. The idea of scale is completely subjectified and the distance becomes a mental, rather abstract distance.

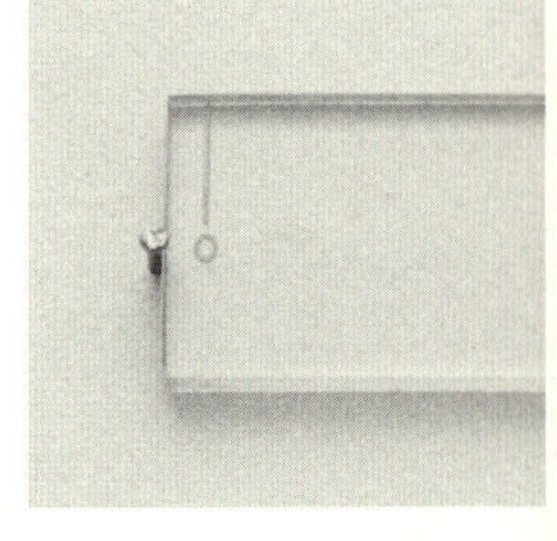

Layout sketch for the first proposal of this book *Studio*, 2008 ›

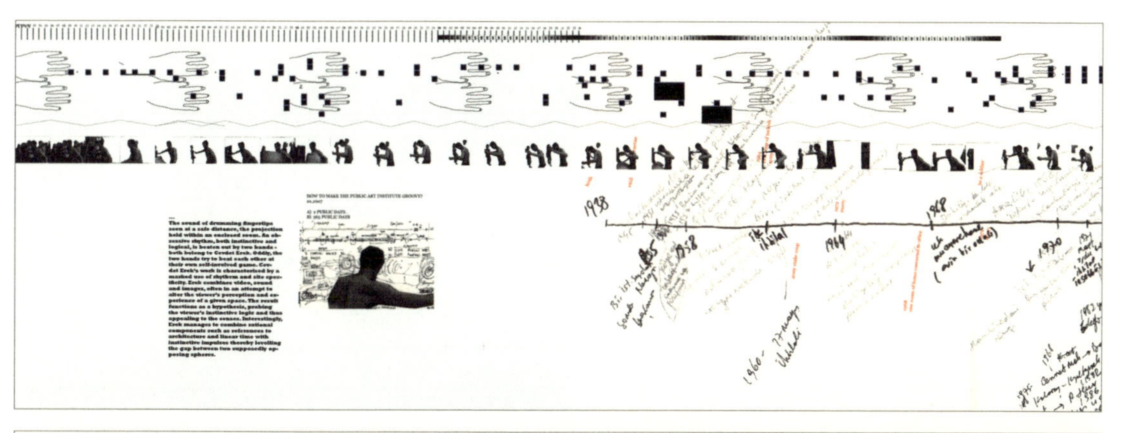

The sound of drumming fingertips seen at a safe distance, the projection held within an enclosed room. An obsessive rhythm, both instinctive and logical, is beaten out by two hands - both belong to Cevdet Erek. Oddly, the two hands try to beat each other at their own self-involved game. Cevdet Erek's work is characterised by a marked use of rhythm and site specificity. Erek combines video, sound and images, often in an attempt to alter the viewer's perception and experience of a given space. The result functions as a hypothesis, probing the viewer's instinctive logic and thus appealing to the senses. Interestingly, Erek manages to combine rational components such as references to architecture and linear time with instinctive impulses thereby levelling the gap between two supposedly opposing spheres.
HOW TO MAKE THE PUBLIC ART INSTITUTE GROOVY?
09.2007
A) 2 PUBLIC DAYS.
B) 365 PUBLIC DAYS

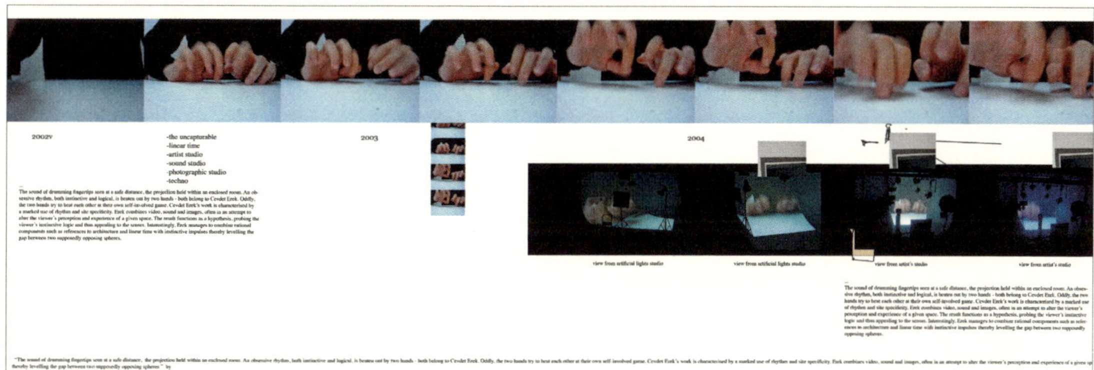

2002v
2003
-the uncapturable
-linear time
-artist studio
-sound studio
-photographic studio
-techno
The sound of drumming fingertips seen at a safe distance, the projection held within an enclosed room. An obsessive rhythm, both instinctive and logical, is beaten out by two hands - both belong to Cevdet Erek. Oddly, the two hands try to beat each other at their own self-involved game. Cevdet Erek's work is characterised by a marked use of rhythm and site specificity. Erek combines video, sound and images, often in an attempt to alter the viewer's perception and experience of a given space. The result functions as a hypothesis, probing the viewer's instinctive logic and thus appealing to the senses. Interestingly, Erek manages to combine rational components such as references to architecture and linear time with instinctive impulses thereby levelling the gap between two supposedly opposing spheres.
2004
view from artificial lights studio
view from artificial lights studio
view from artist's studio
view from artist's studio
The sound of drumming fingertips seen at a safe distance, the projection held within an enclosed room. An obsessive rhythm, both instinctive and logical, is beaten out by two hands - both belong to Cevdet Erek. Oddly, the two hands try to beat each other at their own self-involved game. Cevdet Erek's work is characterised by a marked use of rhythm and site specificity. Erek combines video, sound and images, often in an attempt to alter the viewer's perception and experience of a given space. The result functions as a hypothesis, probing the viewer's instinctive logic and thus appealing to the senses. Interestingly, Erek manages to combine rational components such as references to architecture and linear time with instinctive impulses thereby levelling the gap between two supposedly opposing spheres.
"The sound of drumming fingertips seen at a safe distance, the projection held within an enclosed room. An obsessive rhythm, both instinctive and logical, is beaten out by two hands - both belong to Cevdet Erek. Oddly, thereby levelling the gap between two supposedly opposing spheres." by

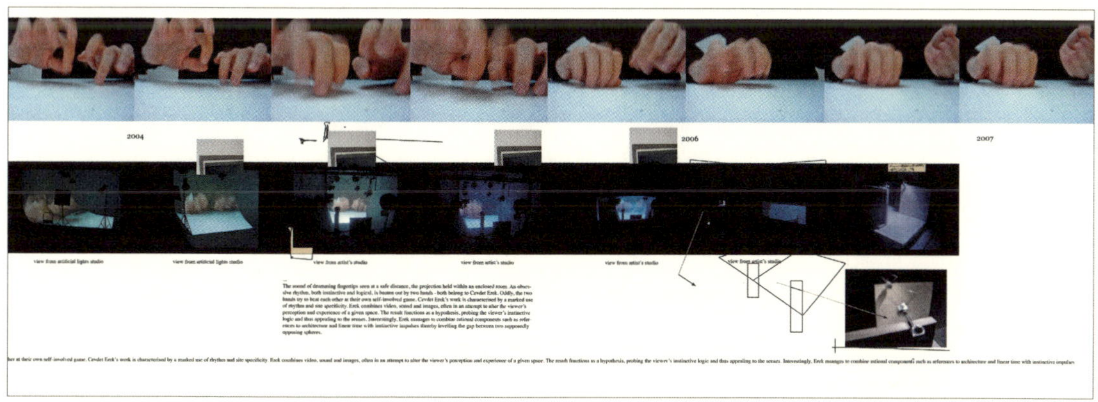

2004
2006
2007
view from artificial lights studio
view from artificial lights studio
view from artist's studio
view from artist's studio
view from artist's studio
view from artist's studio
The sound of drumming fingertips seen at a safe distance, the projection held within an enclosed room. An obsessive rhythm, both instinctive and logical, is beaten out by two hands - both belong to Cevdet Erek. Oddly, the two hands try to beat each other at their own self-involved game. Cevdet Erek's work is characterised by a marked use of rhythm and site specificity. Erek combines video, sound and images, often in an attempt to alter the viewer's perception and experience of a given space. The result functions as a hypothesis, probing the viewer's instinctive logic and thus appealing to the senses. Interestingly, Erek manages to combine rational components such as references to architecture and linear time with instinctive impulses thereby levelling the gap between two supposedly opposing spheres.

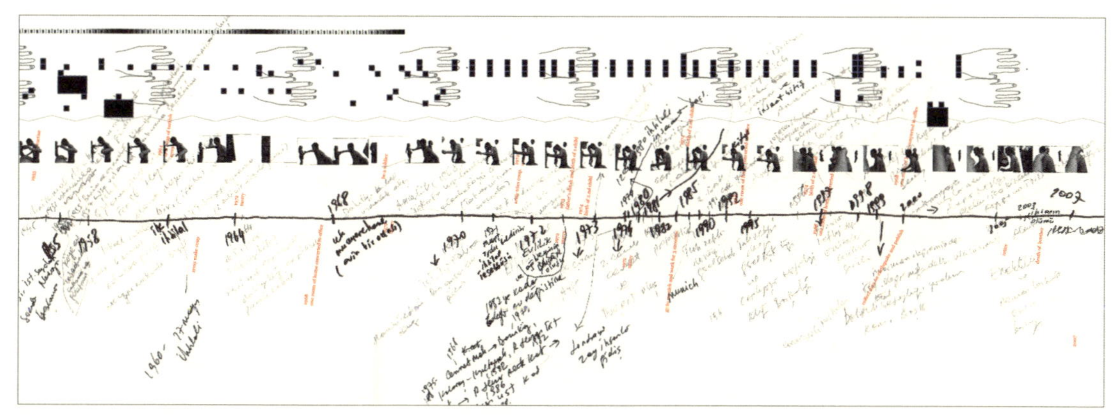

CE: Right. The ruler is fixed, it is constant, a physical material. Its meaning is permanent unless you alter your own perception. A ruler with times on it is a physical thing, but what is on its surface is fluid. In *Ruler 0 - now,* both "0" and "now" are moving; they are in flux. When you try to do this with sound, it is the opposite. The beat flows in time, but it is actually fixed on a loop in an installation. This is a problem of synchronously representing "now" in sound.

With *Ruler 0 - now,* lots of things changed. Scale and years disappeared. In the meantime, I kept producing the initial ruler, the one that started with my birth date, and every time it was produced, the end point advanced to the year it was produced; while it was 2007 when it was made in Cairo, it ended with 2008 in Belgium. When I came back to Istanbul, I made another one with Roman numerals. With every production, the ruler came closer to this moment. But with *Ruler 0-now,* when "now" was put at the end, this was no longer necessary. The now became the moment of the reading.

DD: With "now" you eliminated the physicality. The rulers did not have to literally grow anymore with the passing of years.

CE: I assigned it the length of twenty cm, because I wanted to make a small ruler. When I made it again for the 12th Istanbul Biennial, I made it longer, to make it more spacious, but there is no space after the "now" mark. There is another one that marks "now" and "end." It is similar to *Ruler 0 - now,* again, there is no scale, but there is a new term; the "end."

DD: Maybe it is also important to note that with the 12th Istanbul Biennial, one of the rulers that you made and showed as an art object returned to its functionality as a tool and was produced as a multiple and given away. Can you elaborate on this?

CE: Yes, all of the rulers I have made so far were a means of research and experimentation; they were all presented as prototypes. The aim of their production was for them to be objects or tools that people could hold, take home and hopefully use, rather than to act as objects to be looked at and contemplated in an exhibition setting.

DD: *Ruler I* came out of a time when you experienced the month of Ramadan in Cairo, when you were confronted with an altered sense of time that affects the way one goes about his or her day. And in the work *Day,* the times of prayer determine the exact moments of sunrise and sundown in a particular place. It is the second of your LED works. Maybe this is a good time to mention the first one, *Dark Light Dark...*

CE: *Dark Light Dark* came out of exactly this idea. It follows a simple code of on and off:

dark	light	dark
1	0	1
breakfast	break fast	breakfast
on	off	on

It is about presence and absence. Fasting is not just about not eating; it is the denial or the absence of certain things. No eating, drinking, smoking or alcohol. Absence. Then you eat. You are free during the night. In the code, "1" corresponds to "on," and "0" corresponds to "off." The light is on or off. Similarly to the way we perceive days. During Ramadan, the whole month is a continuous loop of on and off, and it revolves around the sunlight. Dark-light-dark, zero-one-zero or absence-presence-absence.

now

In *Dark Light Dark,* I used Cufic Arabic script on the LED sign. It is similar to bitmap fonts. Cufic is based on a simple grid idea, similar to the pixels on a digital image or screen. I tried to illustrate this idea of presence and absence graphically through Cufic script. The design is multiplied at a half ratio on every line of the screen; it is a kind of geometric ornamentation. On the other hand, it corresponds to different registers of length. And with *Dark Light Dark,* I used movement for the first time. It flowed with time. With this flow, another element entered the equation: speed. How long it takes for the graphic image to flow out of the screen has to be determined. This is the duration of the loop; it can be one second or 20 seconds. This corresponds to tempo or bpm (beats per minute) in music. The LED sign is pixel per second, for instance. *Day* and *Week* came out of this work.

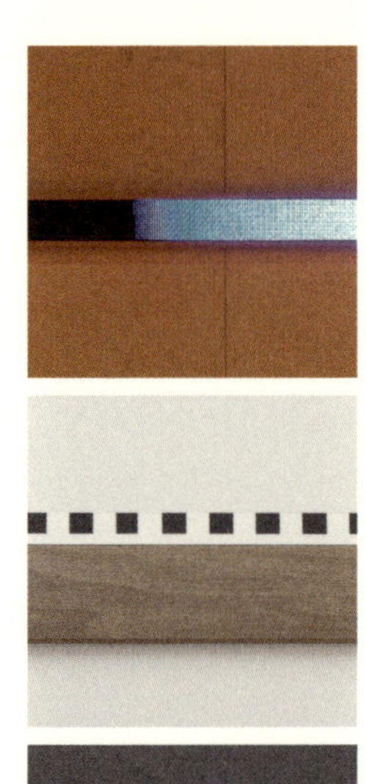

LED is interesting as a material. It is a screen with big pixels; it can be used as a bitmap through pixels or it can be used to show an image. In both *Dark Light Dark* and *Day,* the LED screen is used as an indicator of light and dark.

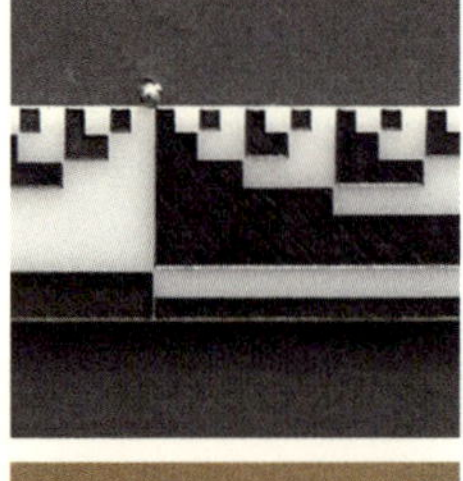

DD: In *Dark Light Dark,* the idea of on and off is applied to Cufic lettering, but there is also an aesthetic choice there, and it has a lot to do with ornamentation.

CE: Yes, it is some sort of formalism perhaps.

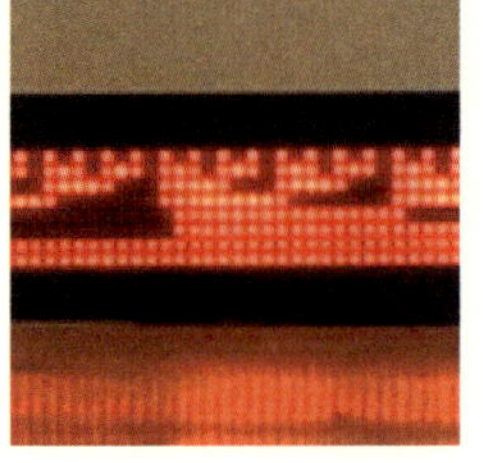

DD: Your works reflect your interest in modernism through your choice of material and their "look." At the same time, you are interested in ornamentation. On one hand, there is a sort of minimalism; simple lines and industrial materials, on the other hand, you sometimes employ ornamentation as a tactic, justifying it with a coding system you apply to it, or at other times you make ornamentation itself the subject of your work. Can we look at some of your projects through this lens? Your work titled *Sky Ornamentation with 3 Sounding Dots and Anti-Pigeon Net* perhaps addresses this on/off relationship you have with ornamentation in your practice. Or there is also *Şaşaa,* the piece you installed on the façade of Arter in 2011.

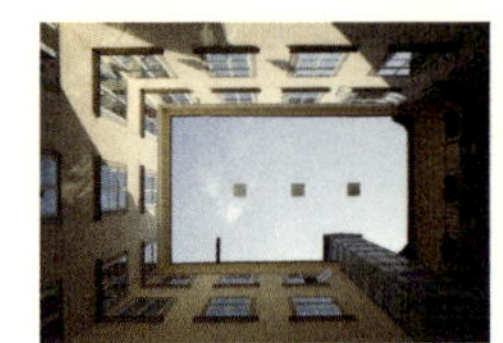

CE: When I went to see the space in Vienna (Thyssen-Bornemisza Art Contemporary) for the first installation of *Tactics of Invisibility,* my interest in courtyards, which I had since I made the work *Avluda (In the Courtyard),* was reawakened. The courtyard is a place that is not an interior space; it is in open air, but at the same time it is located inside a building. Perhaps this is also related to *Week* at Kunsthalle Basel in which I worked with the skylight in the space. It was important to re-consider Adolf Loos's essay *Ornament and Crime* (1908) in the context of *Sky Ornamentation with 3 Sounding Dots and Anti-Pigeon Net.*

As I was dealing with patterns and rhythms and thinking about ornamentation during this time, I wondered whether I could do something about audio-ornamentation. I considered the possibility of creating an audio-ornamentation based on some patterns that would be aesthetically pleasing. This has to do completely with personal taste and is deeply subjective. As I was thinking along these lines, I noticed that in some other courtyards in Vienna they use something called the "anti-pigeon net," which prevents pigeons from soiling courtyards or sculptures and monuments in public space. When I saw the pigeon-nets over the courtyards, I realized that they pixelated the sky, as if it were a screen. This creates an effect with a certain resolution through which you perceive the sky. We installed an anti-pigeon net over the courtyard of TBA21. Then, following the pixels, I used three-directional speakers, which were attached to the anti-pigeon net. The sound piece was titled *3,* and it was structured by basic variations on a ¾ beat, which happens to be a waltz beat. For those of us from Turkey, it is the rhythm of *semai,* which came to Istanbul from Vienna. Since I was creating ornamentation and using a

 Sky Ornamentation with 3 Sounding Dots and Anti-Pigeon Net (SO3SDAPN), 2010 ›

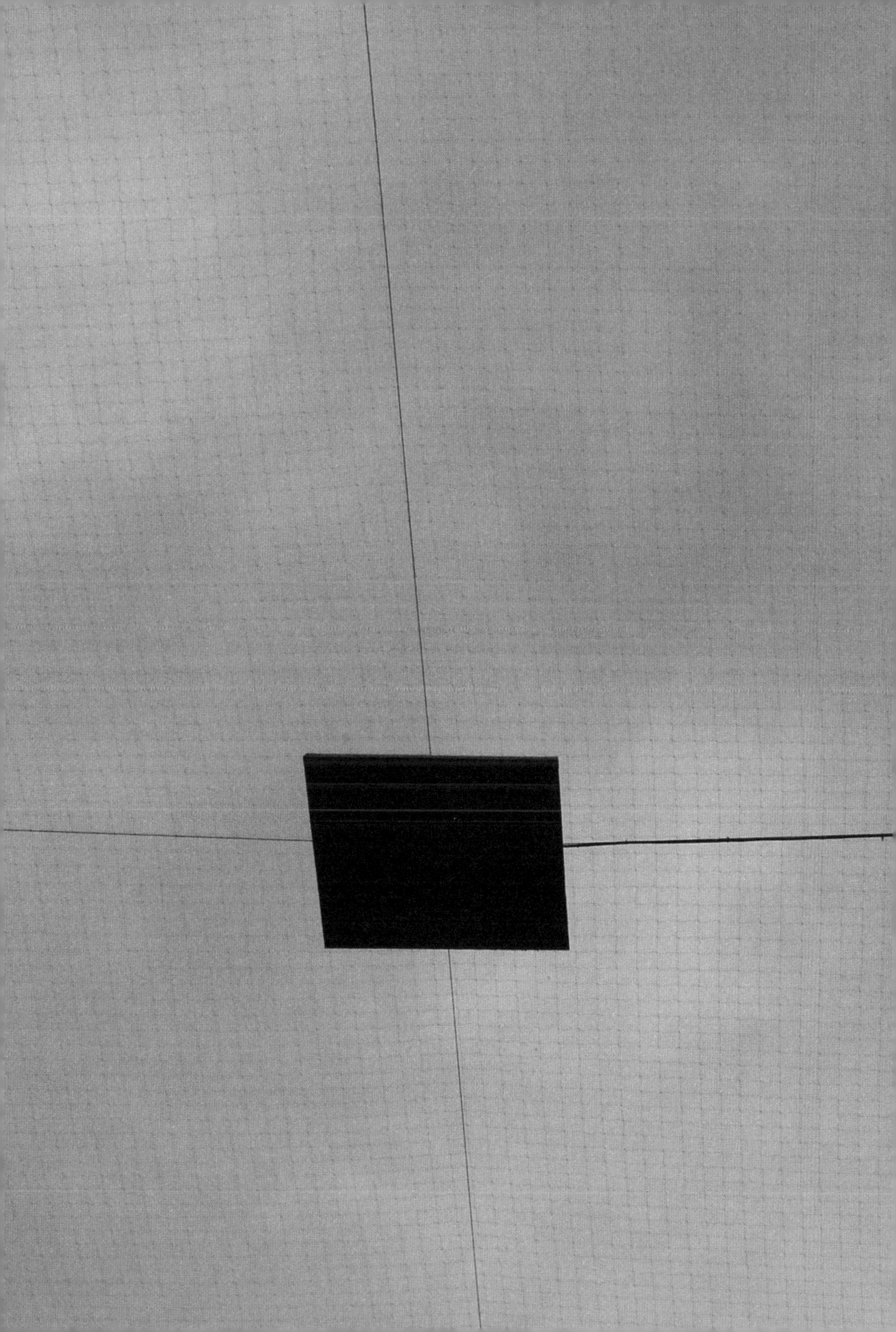

rhythm that refers to a dance, I programmed the three speakers to play variations
of this rhythm; it is not necessarily a meaningful rhythm. This created three patterns, of which visitors would hear echoes when they entered the courtyard. You
could hear them individually when you stood under each directional speaker. The
work was hence titled *Sky Ornamentation with 3 Sounding Dots and Anti-Pigeon
Net*. Since this was a touring exhibition, in its second installation, it became *Kolon
at Tanas*, which was completely different. And at its third and final stop, at Arter,
I came back to visual ornamentation.

Arter is located in a late 19th/early 20th century building in Pera, which has been
a prosperous neighborhood and a dynamic economical and cultural center since
the 1850s; its architectural language refers to a formal urban westernization.
There is a sense of splendor, psychologically if not visually, in terms of the building as well as the institution. The title of this work was *Şaşaa*, an onomatopoeia,
which means splendor. *Şaşaa* perhaps is a translated echo of shiny surfaces, as
they are reflective. I was in the midst of making another work with LED signs,
busy with creating forms out of the small bits that form the letters in LED text
displays, and the idea of using all the elements of the LED sign to create a so-
called ornamentation emerged. I wouldn't be creating an image out of the parts
of letters, but would be providing the full scope of them, and the pedestrians on
the street would create the image by taking away the pixels, which in this case
were stickers. I provoked this by taking a few out myself at first. So, a kind of ornamentation would form by chance over time, as people took stickers off, and it
would also eventually disappear on its own. It was a kind of ornamentation that
was not static; it changed over time. The individual stickers had lives of their own
afterwards. And the pattern came from an LED sign to begin with. Inside the
exhibition space, I installed one of the speakers I had used in Vienna on a wall, in
addition to the LED sign, which showed an animated and time-based version of
the pattern-based ornament outside on eight modules of LED.

DD: How does *RoR* benefit from the ideas in your previous works? And how does
it differ from these experiments, what is new? Is there perhaps a thread running
through all of them that is embodied in *RoR* in a different language?

CE: First and foremost, this book as well as a few earlier attempts at organiza-
tion/documentation of related work forced me to revisit, remember and re-read
all the work before and during the phases of development and realization of *RoR*.
There have been so many attempts (most of which, I would say, are noise) in the
last few years — or even decade — that I can't remember the processes and lessons
learned from some of the works. In this regard, documentation helps immensely.

Secondly, *RoR* is a proposal for an all-encompassing experience for a defined duration in a defined place, including its memory, what is outside, the pathway to it,
its signage, plan etc. Practically, *RoR* is a spatial configuration, architectural and
beyond. It is an overall strategy for a central soundscape and surrounding local
soundscapes, with many other details. Most of what comprises *RoR* is in part the
result of past experiments. This is probably the main benefit.

I think it is too early to say what is new or different in *RoR*, as I just started learn-
ing from the piece. But what I can say is that this is a standalone work. *RoR* has
clearly established its own place and time, or a multiplicity of times, in a city, with
a single proposal; it is built up of a hundred sub-proposals, it is a reality of its
own, surrounded by other realities.

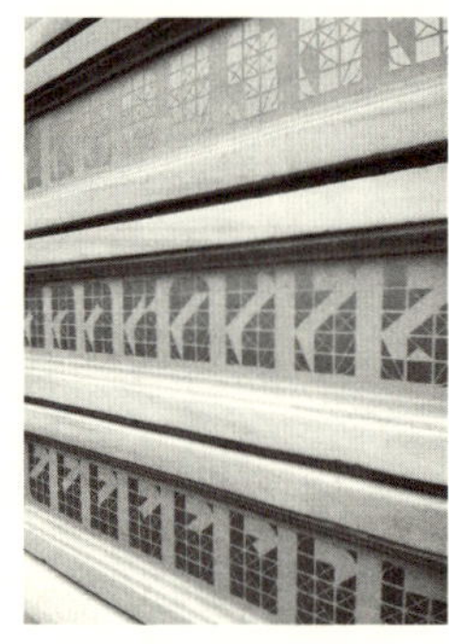

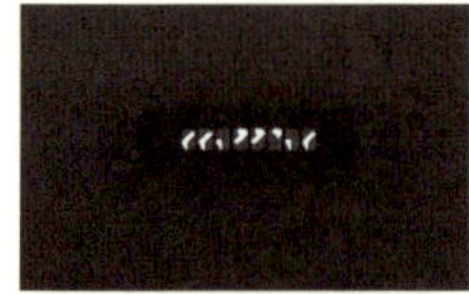

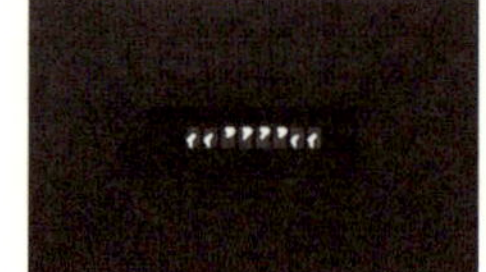

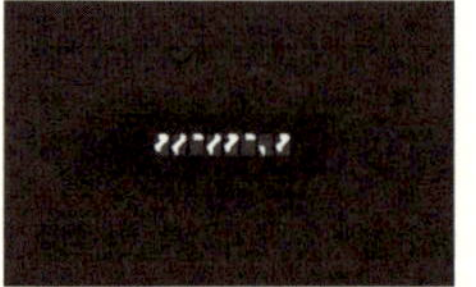

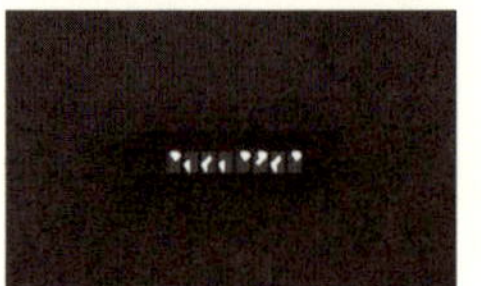

Installation view of *Şaşaa*, façade of ARTER, Space for Art, Istanbul, 2011 ˄
View from *Variations on the Rhythms of Room of Rhythms*
during the performance, dOCUMENTA (13), July 13th, 2012 ˃

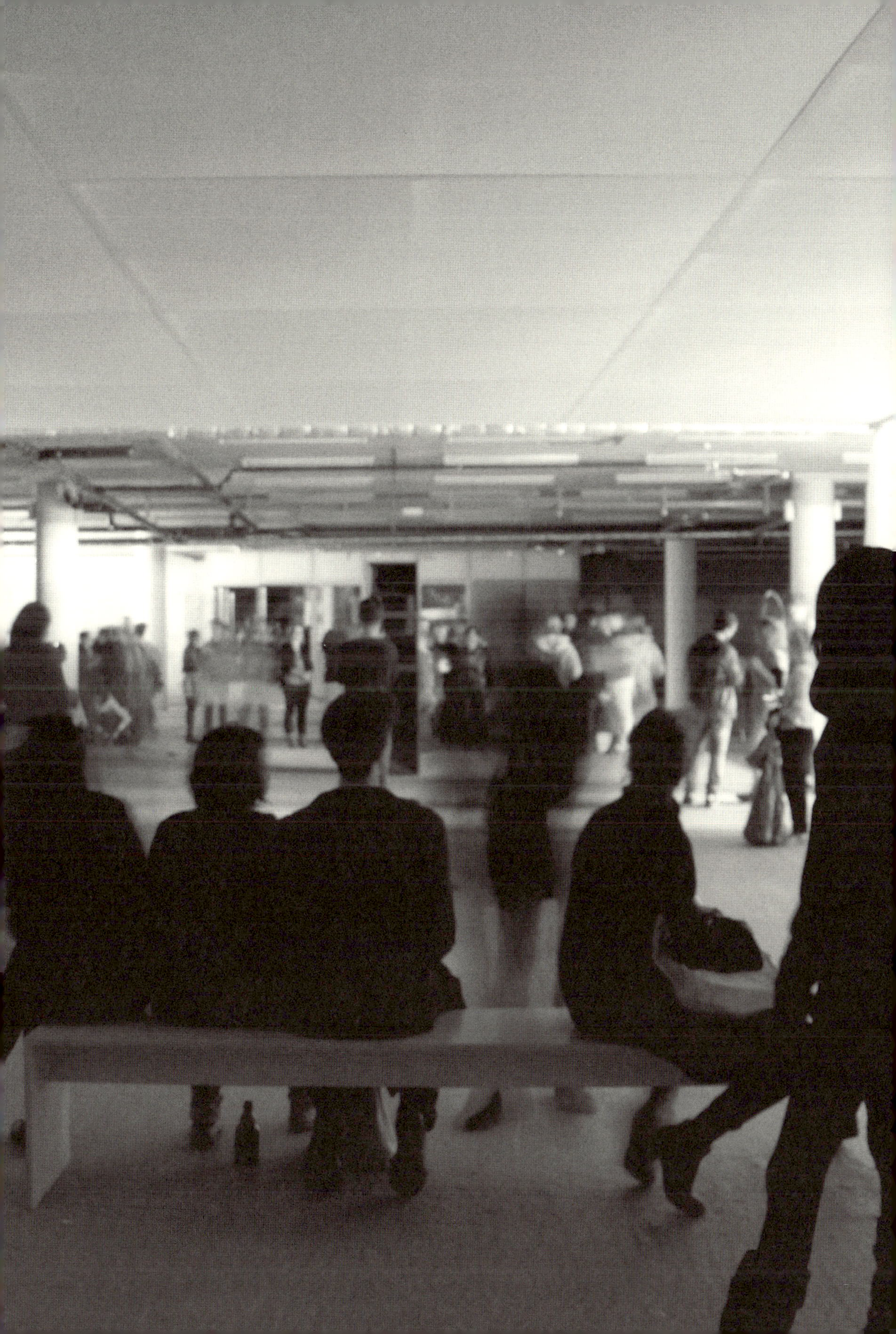

Room of Rhythms

International Style

60 bpm

Reduction Forever

Chronocracy

Culture of anniversary

Arrhythmie

This part is closed on sundays.

Please come later.

Scale:
1 day = 1 second
1 day = 1 window

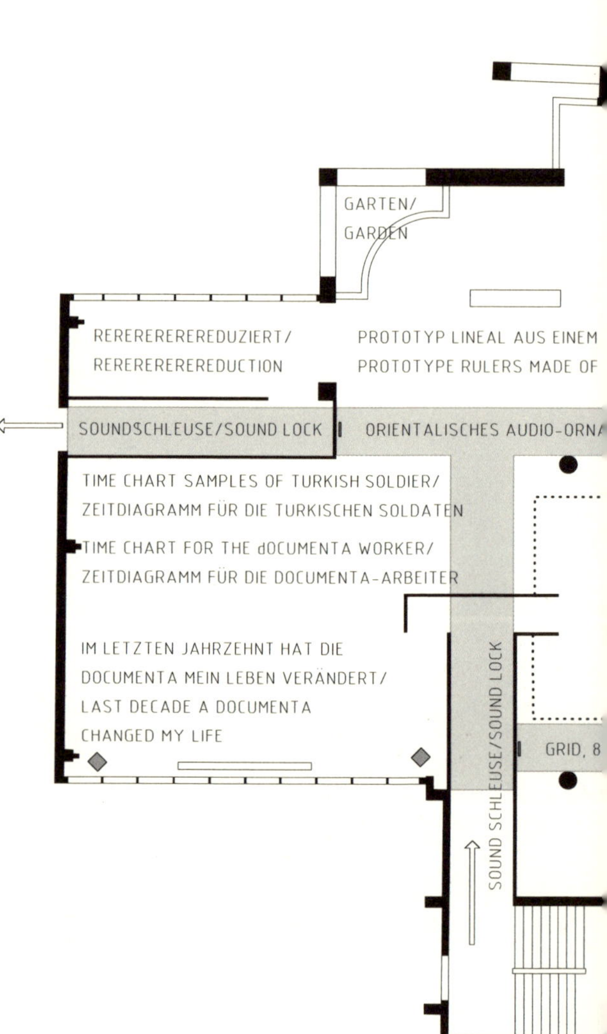

Map, *Room of Rhythms* at dOCUMENTA (13), 2012

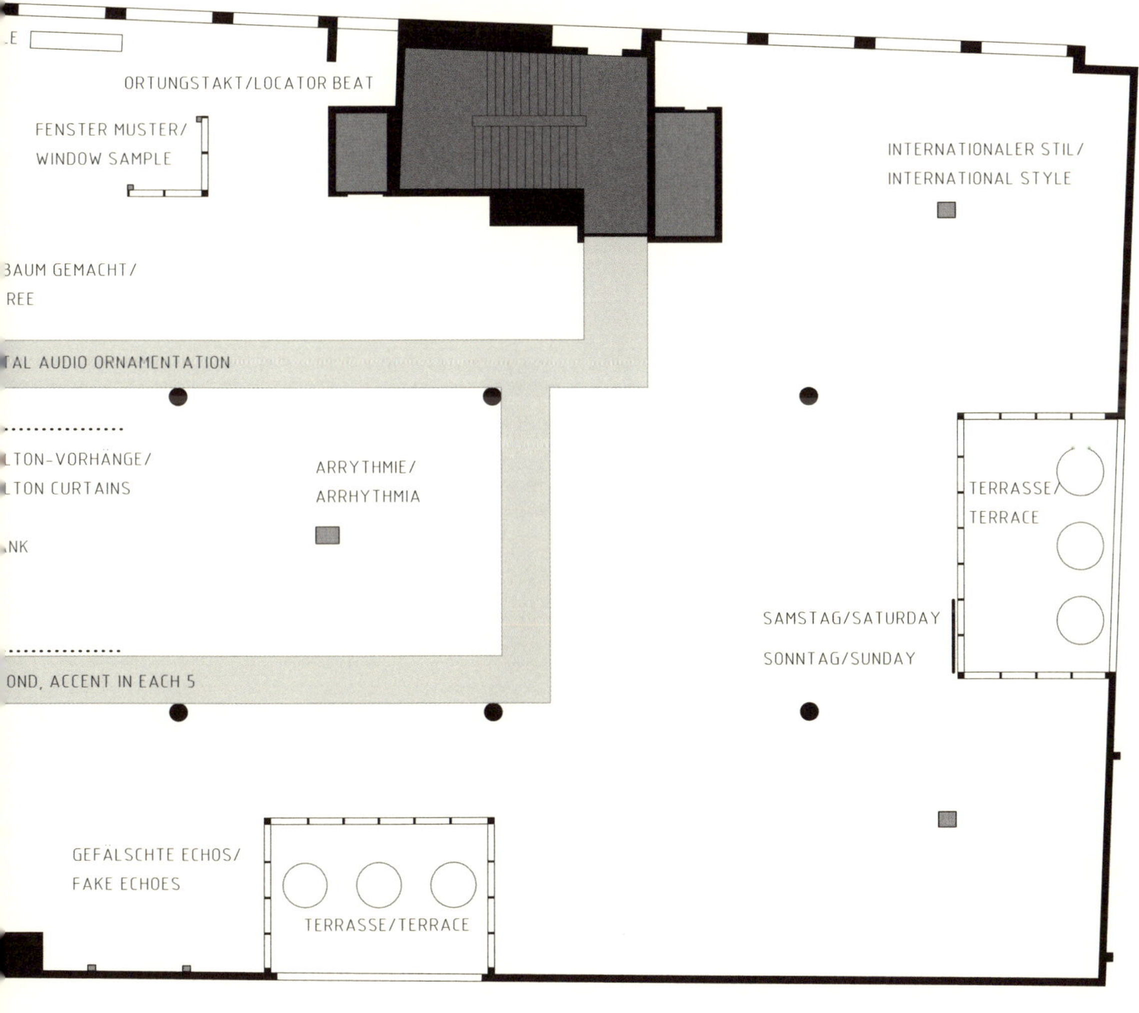
ORTUNGSTAKT/LOCATOR BEAT
FENSTER MUSTER/
WINDOW SAMPLE
INTERNATIONALER STIL/
INTERNATIONAL STYLE
BAUM GEMACHT/
REE
TAL AUDIO ORNAMENTATION
TON-VORHÄNGE/
TON CURTAINS
ARRYTHMIE/
ARRHYTHMIA
NK
TERRASSE/
TERRACE
SAMSTAG/SATURDAY
SONNTAG/SUNDAY
OND, ACCENT IN EACH 5
GEFÄLSCHTE ECHOS/
FAKE ECHOES
TERRASSE/TERRACE

  Map, *SWCS (Stedelijk Waterfalls CS)*, Stedelijk Museum Amsterdam, 2006

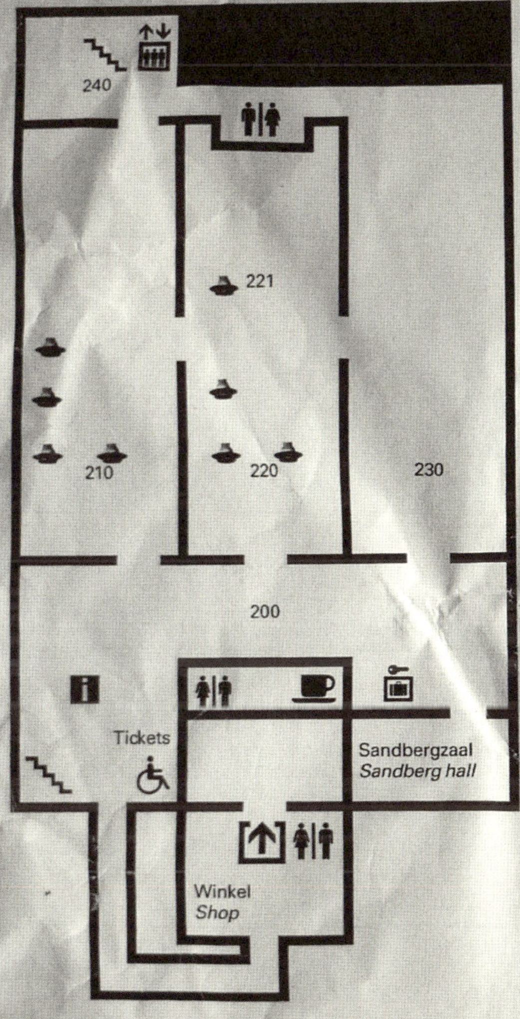

Stedelijk Waterfalls CS

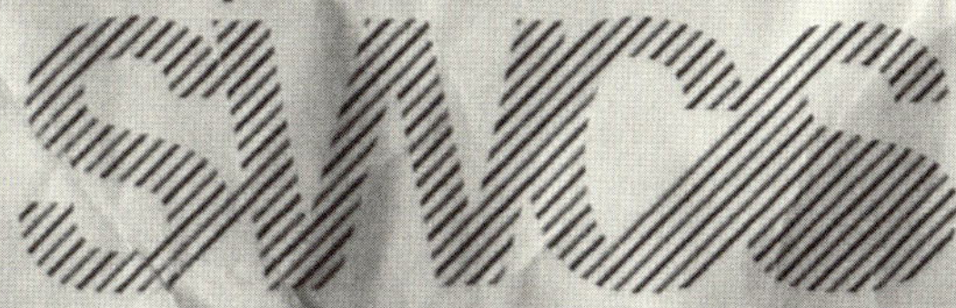

Stedelijk Museum CS

Oosterdokskade 5
1011 AD Amsterdam

Open: 10-18 h
www.stedelijk.nl

     Handout, *4/4 (Nekropsi proudly tries)*, 2007

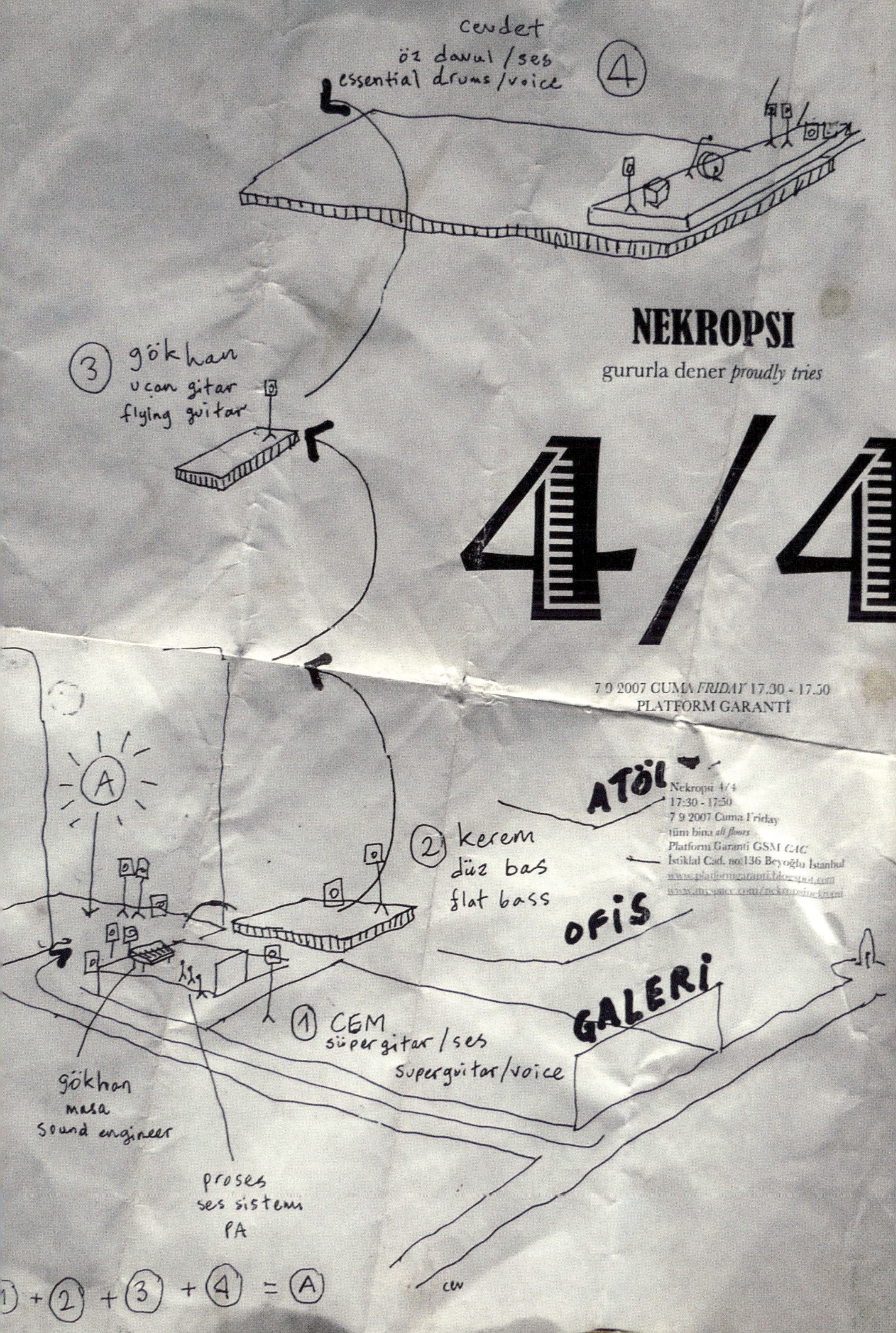

cevdet
öz davul / ses
essential drums / voice
④
NEKROPSI
gururla dener proudly tries
4/4
7 9 2007 CUMA FRIDAY 17.30 - 17.50
PLATFORM GARANTİ
③ gökhan
uçan gitar
flying guitar
② kerem
düz bas
flat bass
① CEM
süper gitar / ses
superguitar / voice
ATÖL~
OFIS
GALERİ
Nekropsi 4/4
17:30 - 17:50
7 9 2007 Cuma Friday
tüm bina all floors
Platform Garanti GSM CAC
İstiklal Cad. no:136 Beyoğlu İstanbul
www.platformgaranti.blogspot.com
www.myspace.com/nekropsinekropsi
gökhan
masa
sound engineer
proses
ses sistemi
PA
① + ② + ③ + ④ = Ⓐ
cw

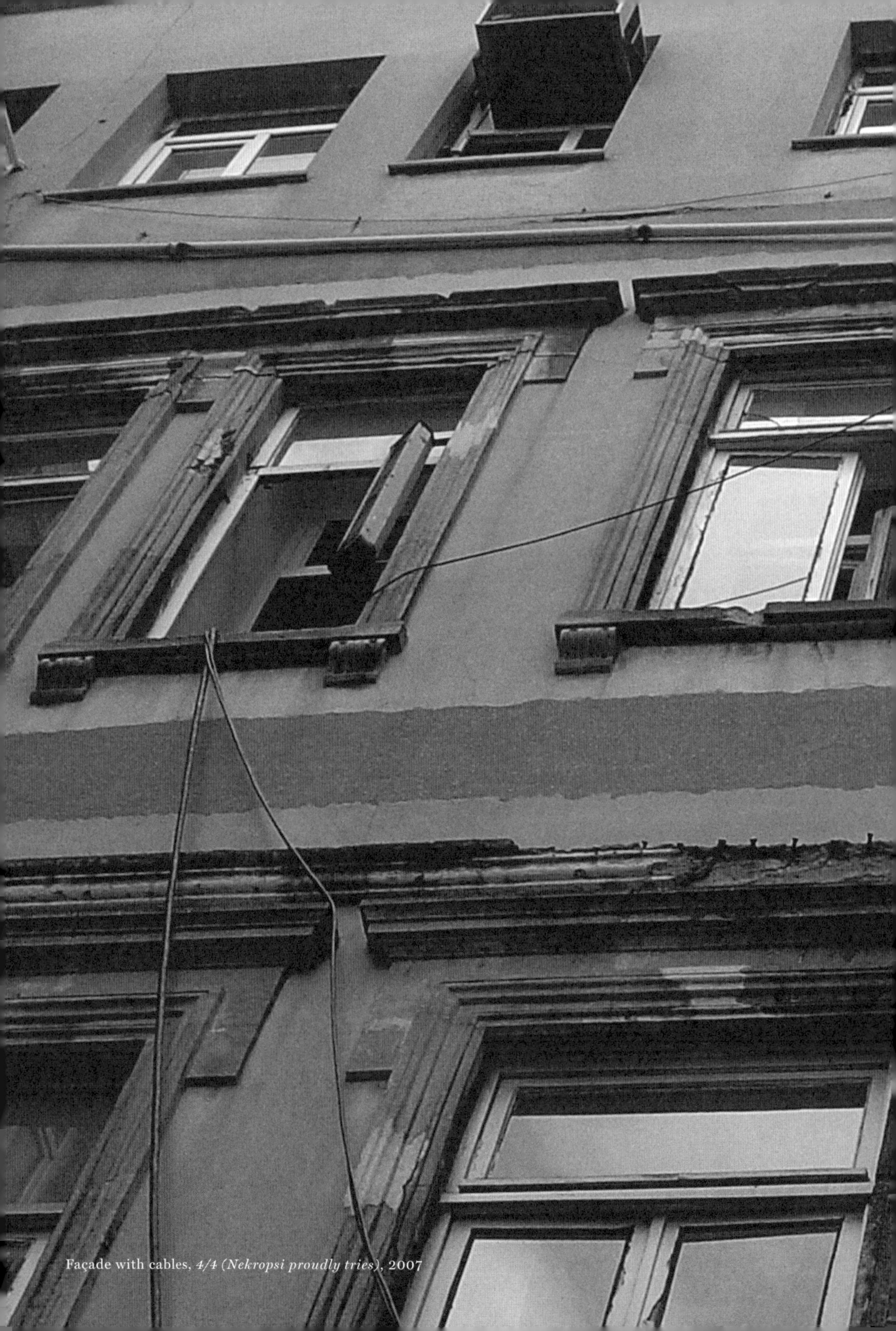

Façade with cables, *4/4 (Nekropsi proudly tries)*, 2007

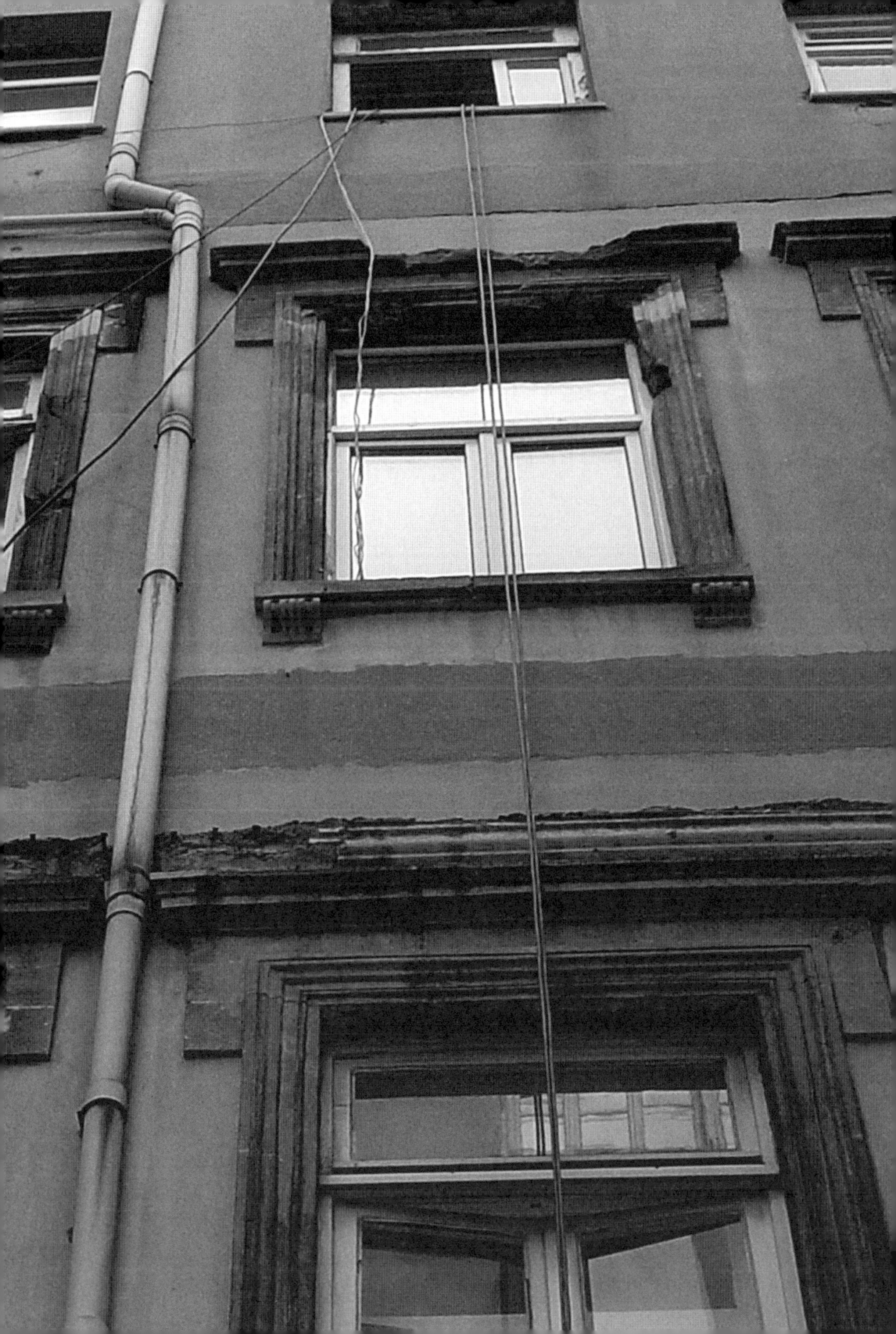

1	2	3	4
5	6	7	8
9	10	11	12
13	14	15	16
17	18	19	20
21	22	23	24
25	26	27	28
29	30	31	32
33	34	35	36
40	41	42	43
47	48	49	50
54	55	56	57

37	38	39
44	45	46
51	52	53
58	59	60

61	62	63	64	65	66	67	68	69	70
71	72	73	74	75	76	77	78	79	80
81	82	83	84	85	86	87	88	89	90
91	92	93	94	95	96	97	98	99	100

101	102	103
104	105	106
107	108	109
110	111	112

113	114	115	116
123	124	125	126
133	134	135	136
143	144	145	146
153	154	155	156
163	164	165	166
173	174	175	176
180	181	182	183
187	188	189	190
191	192	193	194
195	196	197	198
199	200	201	202
209	210	211	212
219	220	221	222
227	228	229	230
235	236	237	238
243	244	245	246
251	252	253	254
259	260	261	262
269	270	271	272

119	120	121	122
129	130	131	132
139	140	141	142
149	150	151	152
159	160	161	162
169	170	171	172
	177	178	179
	184	185	186
205	206	207	208
215	216	217	218
223	224	225	226
231	232	233	234
239	240	241	242
247	248	249	250
255	256	257	258
265	266	267	268
275	276	277	278

279	280	281	282	283	284	285	286	287	288
289	290	291	292	293	294	295	296	297	298
299	300	301	302	303	304	305	306	307	308
309	310	311	312	313	314	315	316	317	318
319	320	321	322	323	324	325	326	327	328
329	330	331	332			333	334	335	336
337	338	339	340			341	342	343	344
345	346	347	348			349	350	351	352
353	354	355	356			357	358	359	360
361	362	363	364			365	366	367	368
369	370	371	372			373	374	375	376
377	378	379	380			381	382	383	384
385	386	387	388			389	390	391	392
393	394	395	396			397	398	399	400
401	402	403	404	405	406	407	408	409	410
411	412	413	414	415	416	417	418	419	420
421	422	423	424	425	426	427	428	429	430
431	432	433	434	435	436	437	438	439	440
441	442	443	444	445	446	447	448	449	450
451	452	453	454	455	456	457	458	459	460

http://ergin53.bildirgec.org/

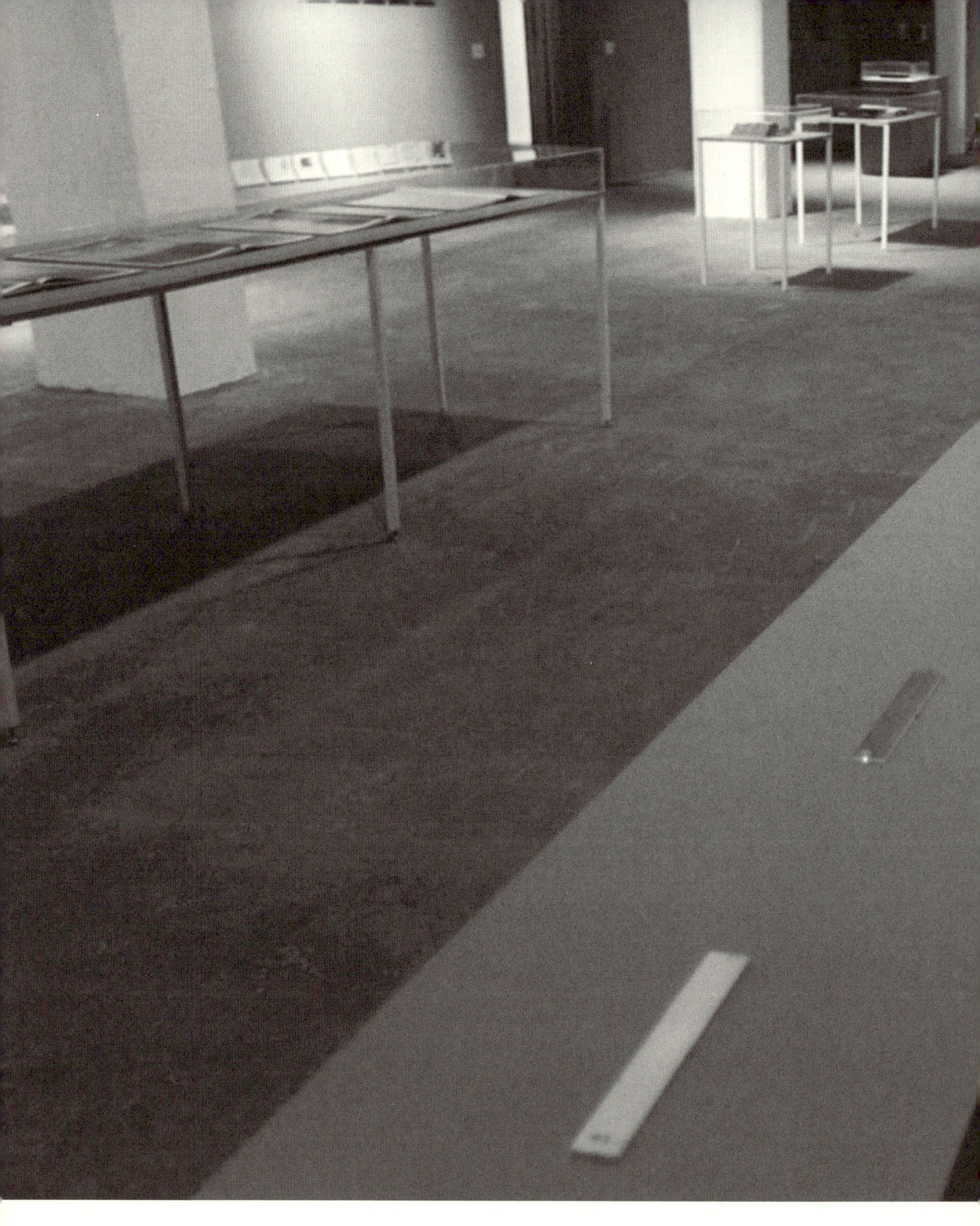

   Installation view and installation plan of *Rulers and Rhythm Studies, Untitled (12th Istanbul Biennial)*, 2011

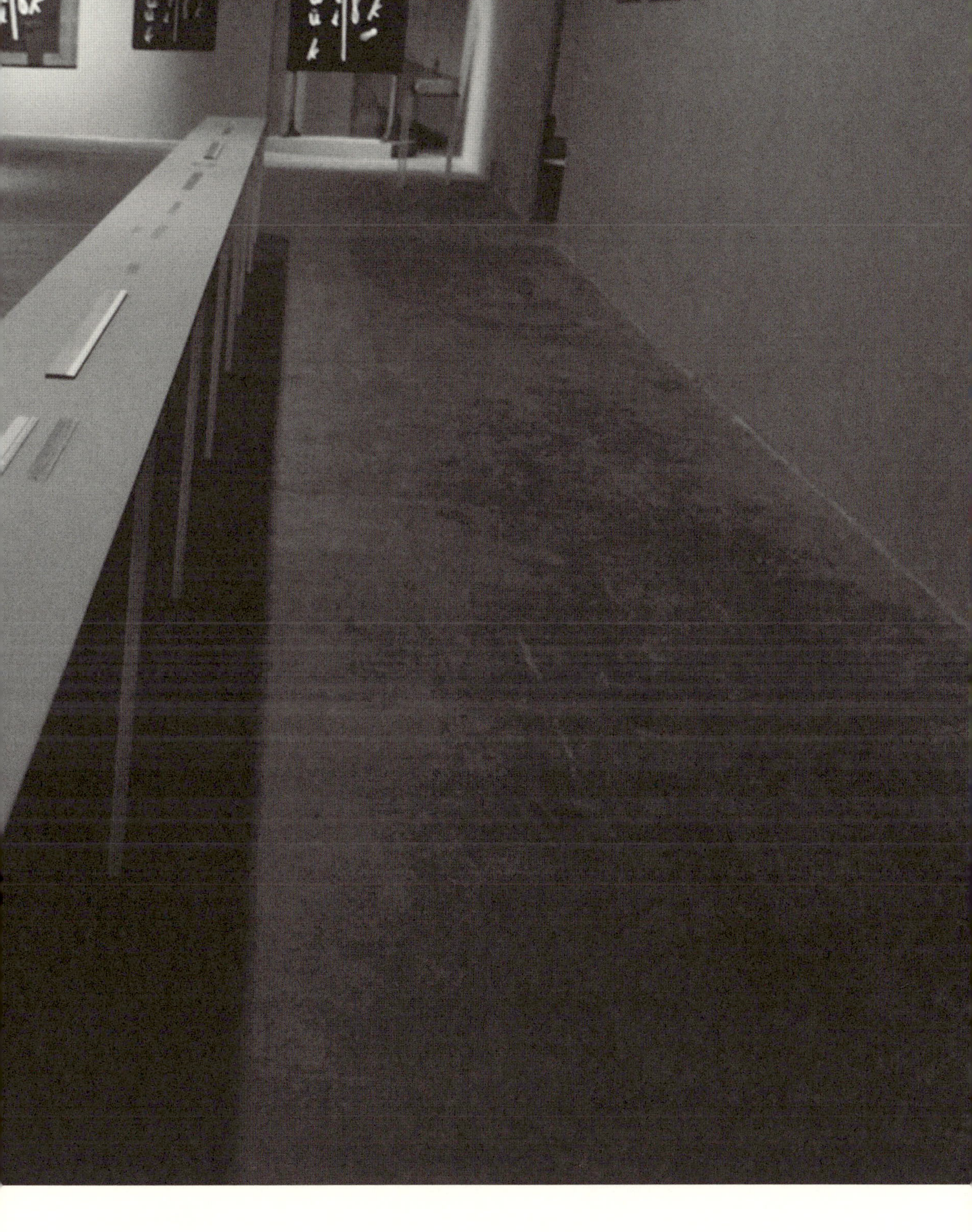

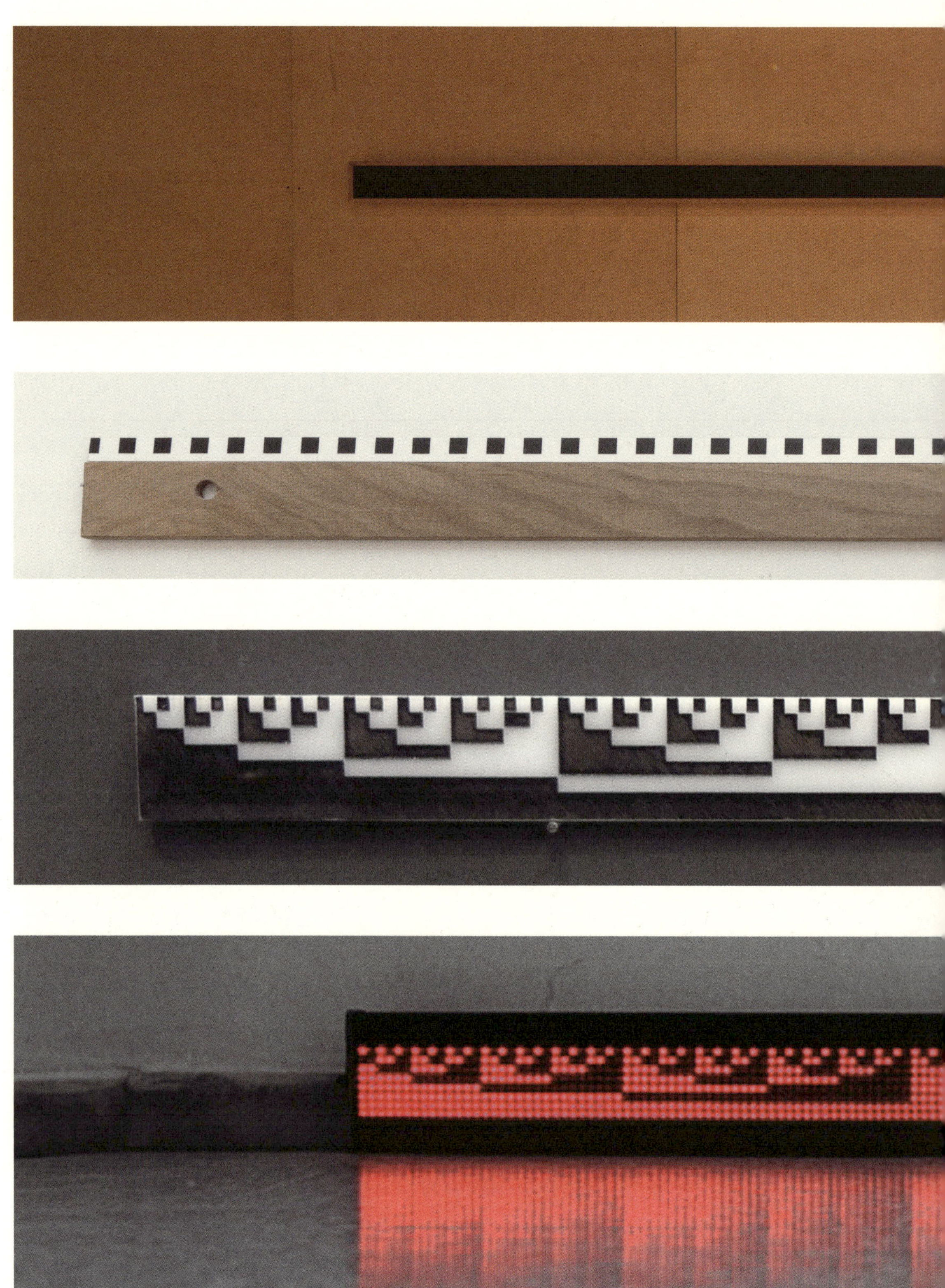

  From top: *Day*, 2011; *Ruler Day Night*, 2011; *Dark Light Dark*, panel, 2007; *Dark Light Dark*, LED, 2007

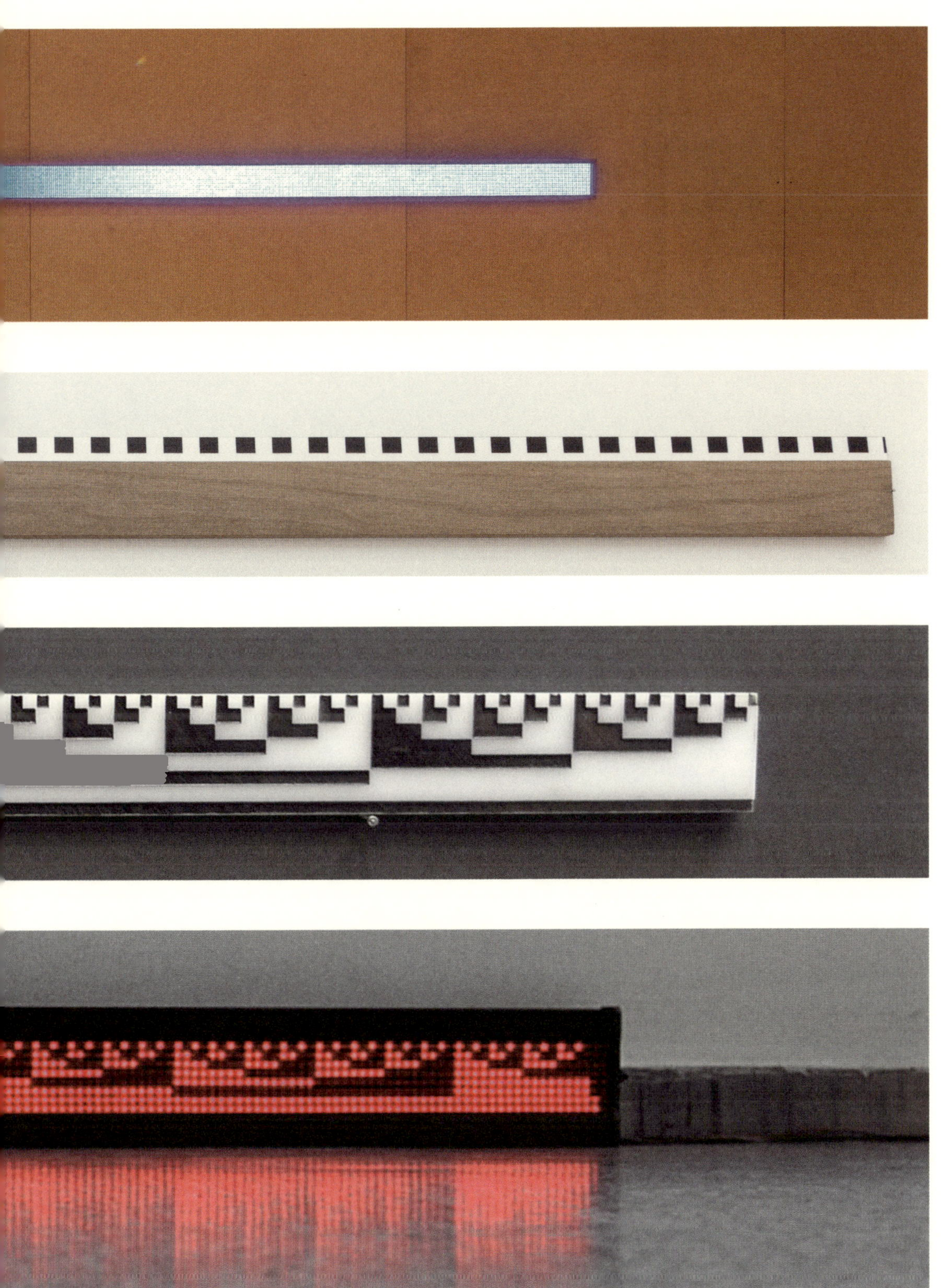

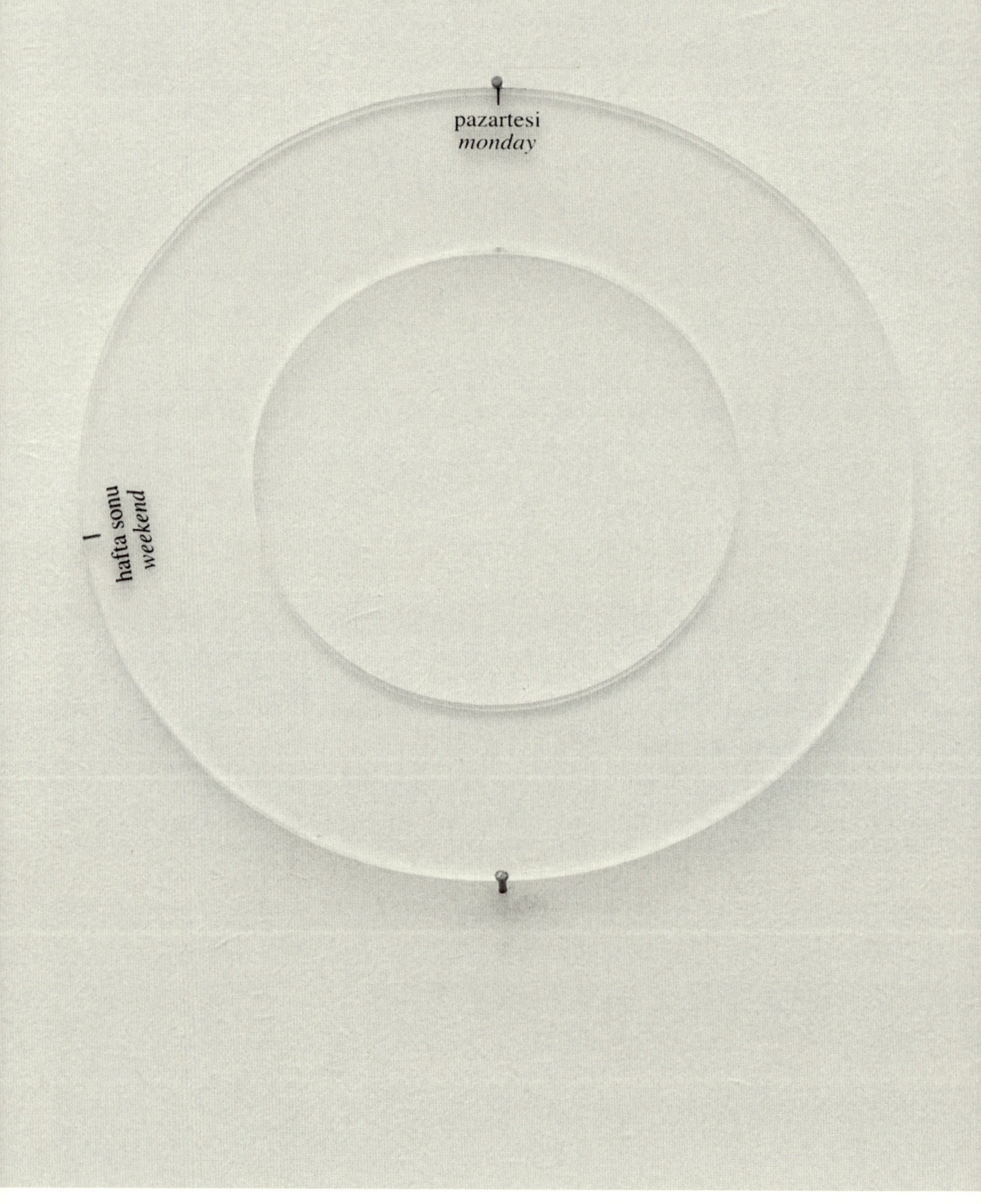

  Circular Week Ruler, 2011 ^
Circular Week Ruler & 7, ruler on table and directional loudspeaker, 2011 >

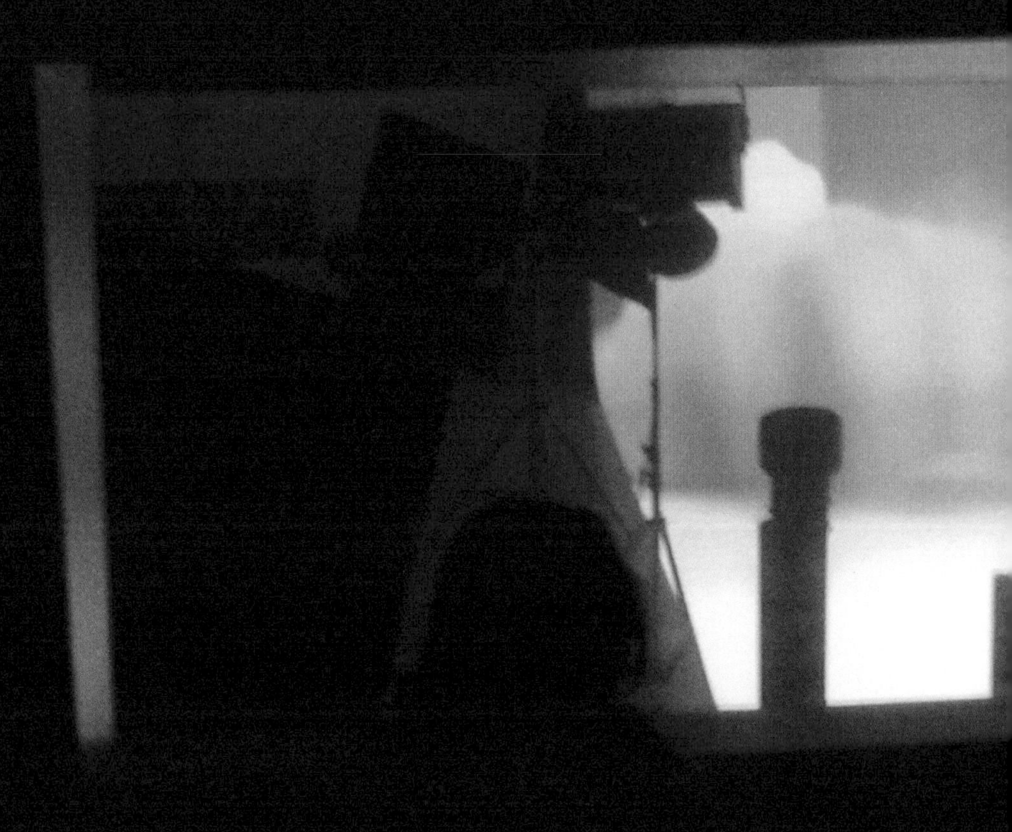

Installation view from *Studio*, Rijksakademie Amsterdam, 2005

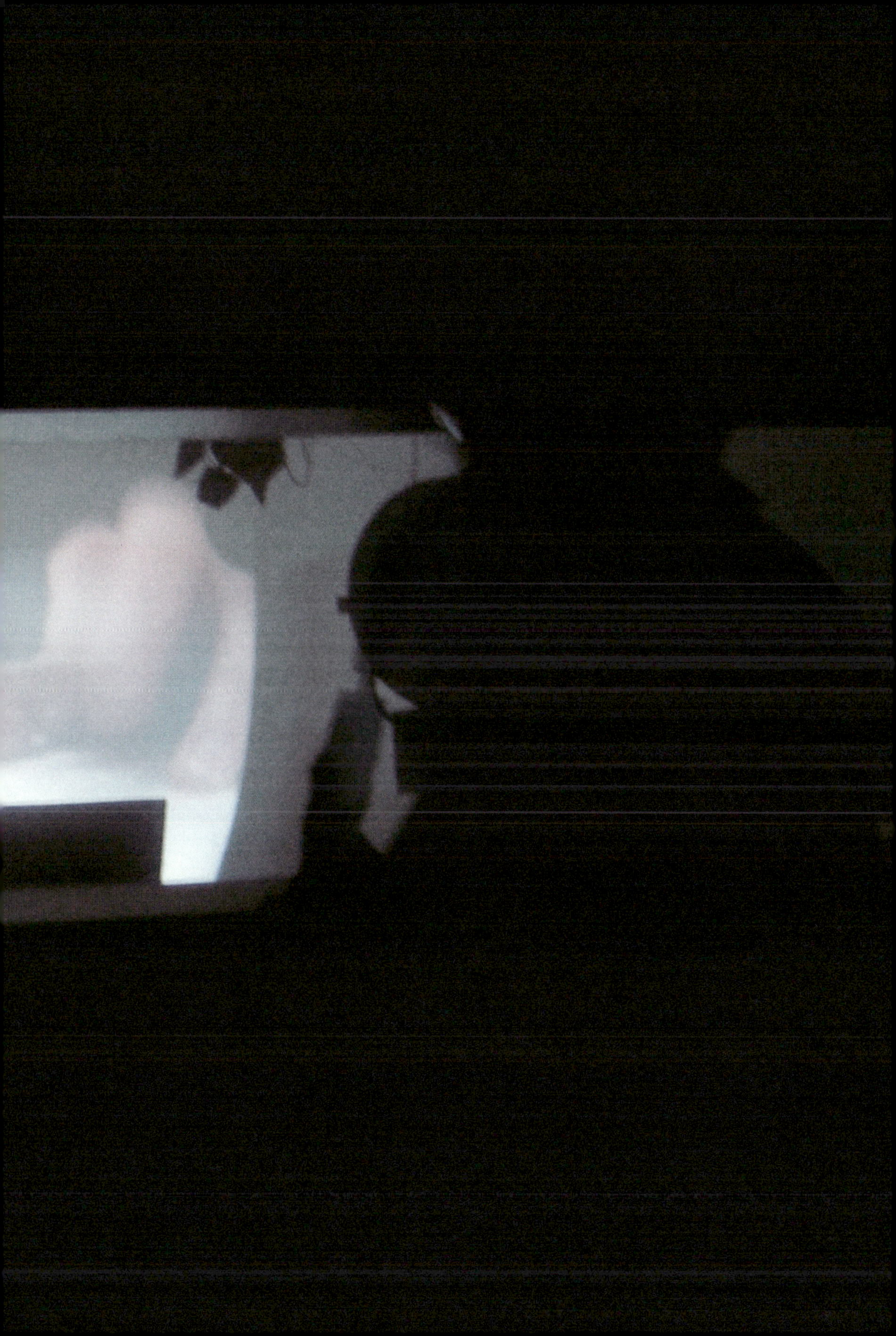

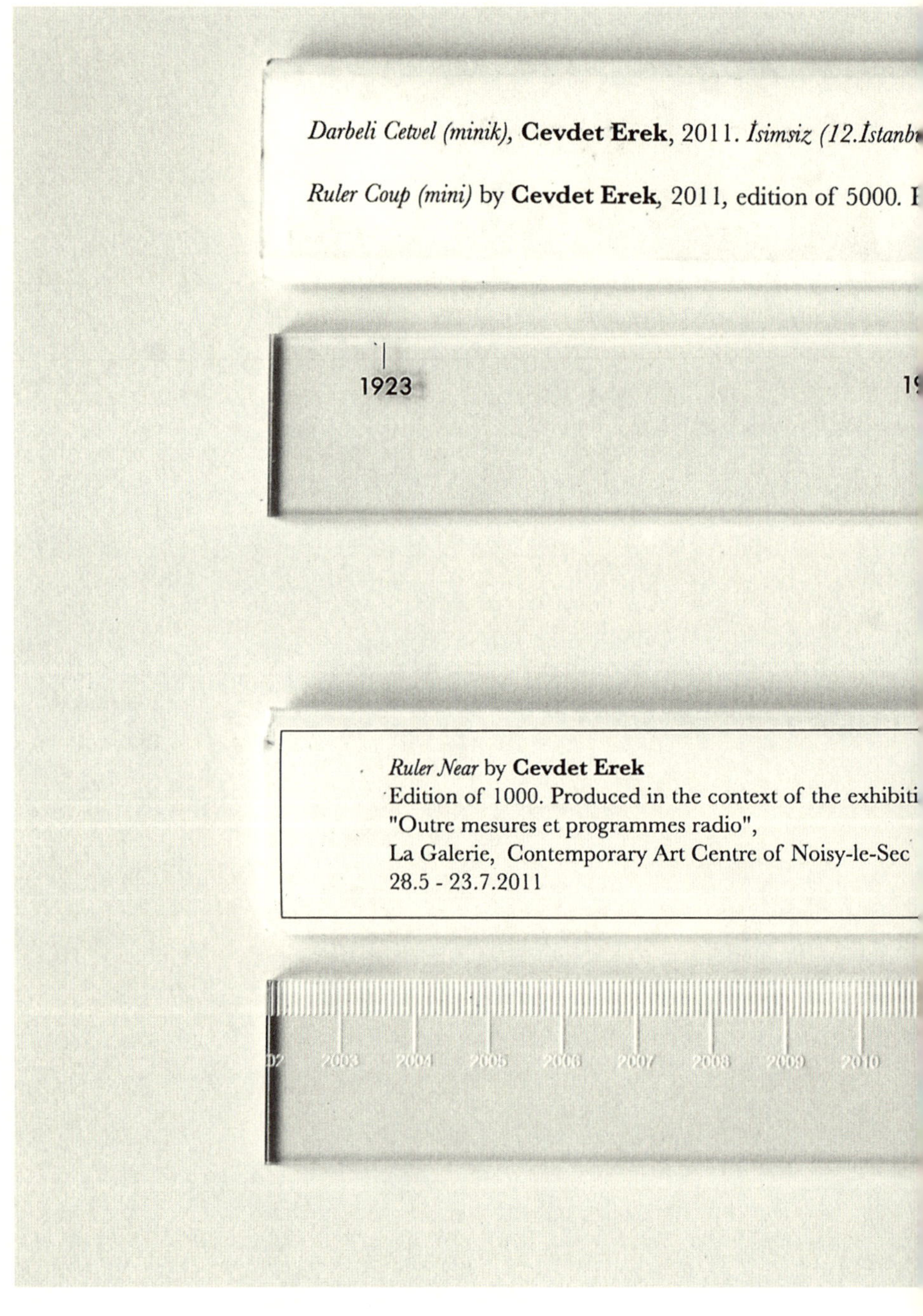

Darbeli Cetvel (minik), Cevdet Erek, 2011. İsimsiz (12.İstanb
Ruler Coup (mini) by Cevdet Erek, 2011, edition of 5000. I
1923
19
Ruler Near by Cevdet Erek
Edition of 1000. Produced in the context of the exhibiti
"Outre mesures et programmes radio",
La Galerie, Contemporary Art Centre of Noisy-le-Sec
28.5 - 23.7.2011
2003   2004   2005   2006   2007   2008   2009   2010

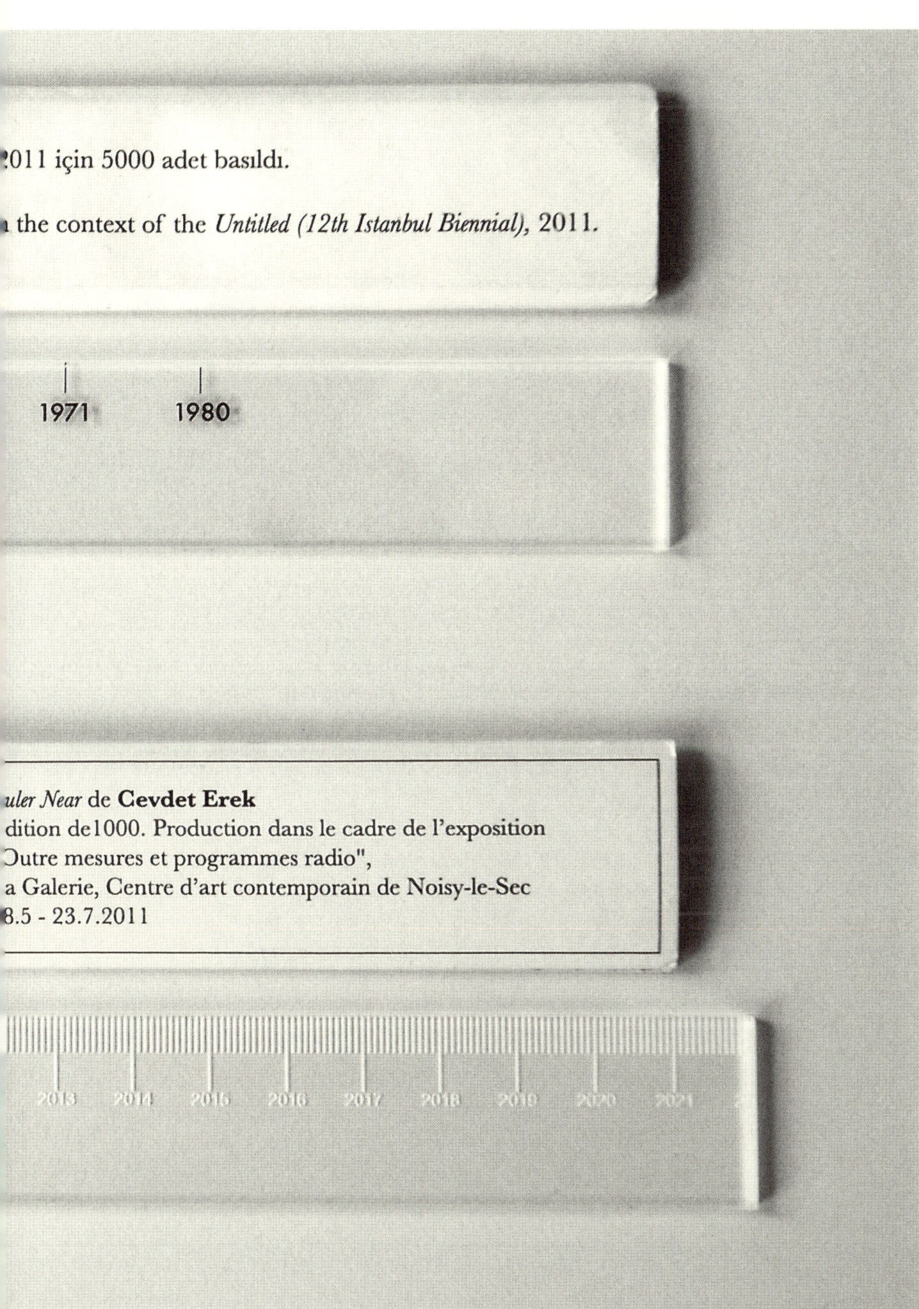

?011 için 5000 adet basıldı.

a the context of the *Untitled (12th Istanbul Biennial), 2011.*

1971   1980

uler *Near* de **Cevdet Erek**
dition de1000. Production dans le cadre de l'exposition
Outre mesures et programmes radio",
a Galerie, Centre d'art contemporain de Noisy-le-Sec
8.5 - 23.7.2011

2013   2014   2015   2016   2017   2018   2019   2020   2021

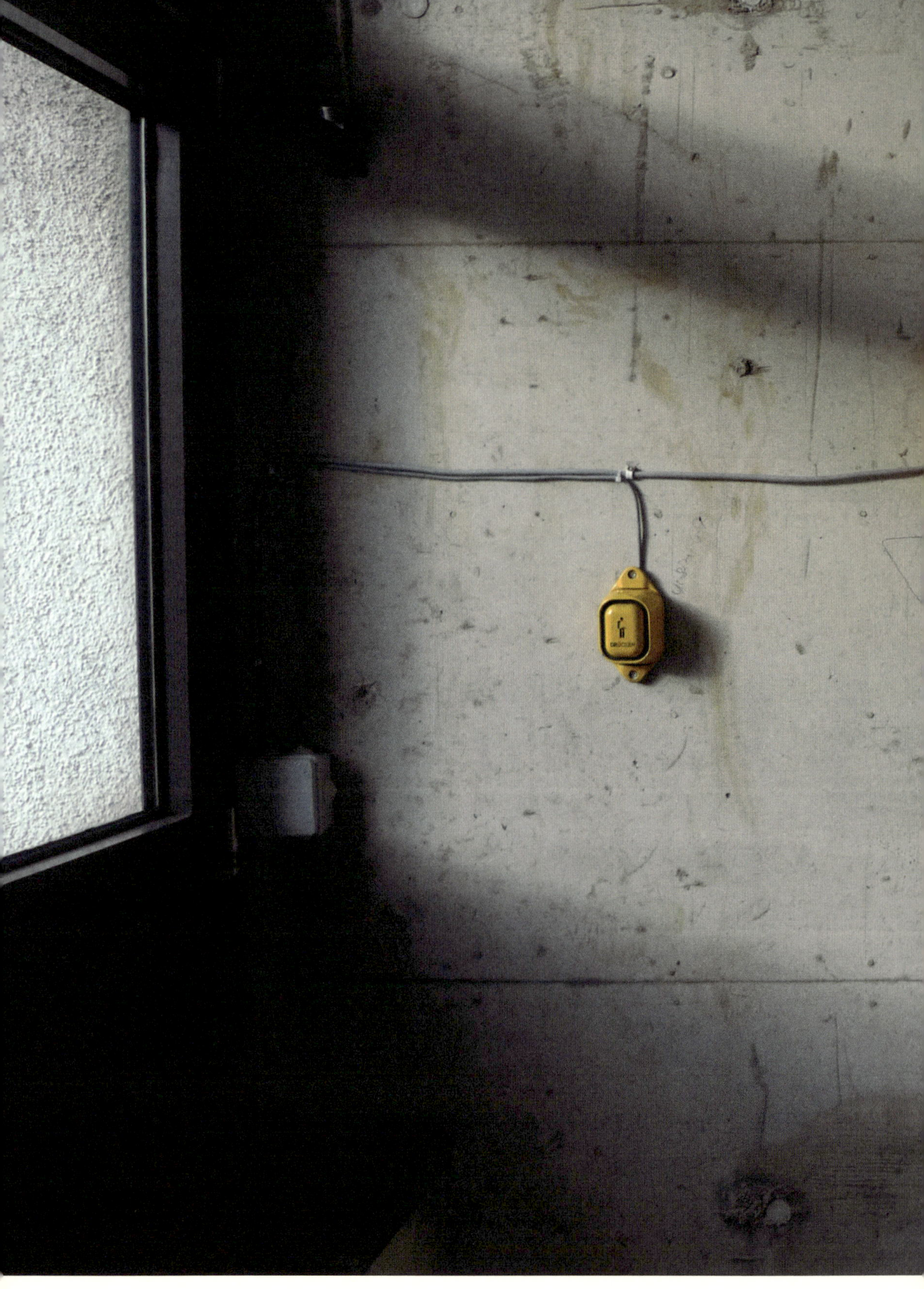

70   Traffic light beeper, button and sign, *Room of Rhythms*, dOCUMENTA (13), 2012

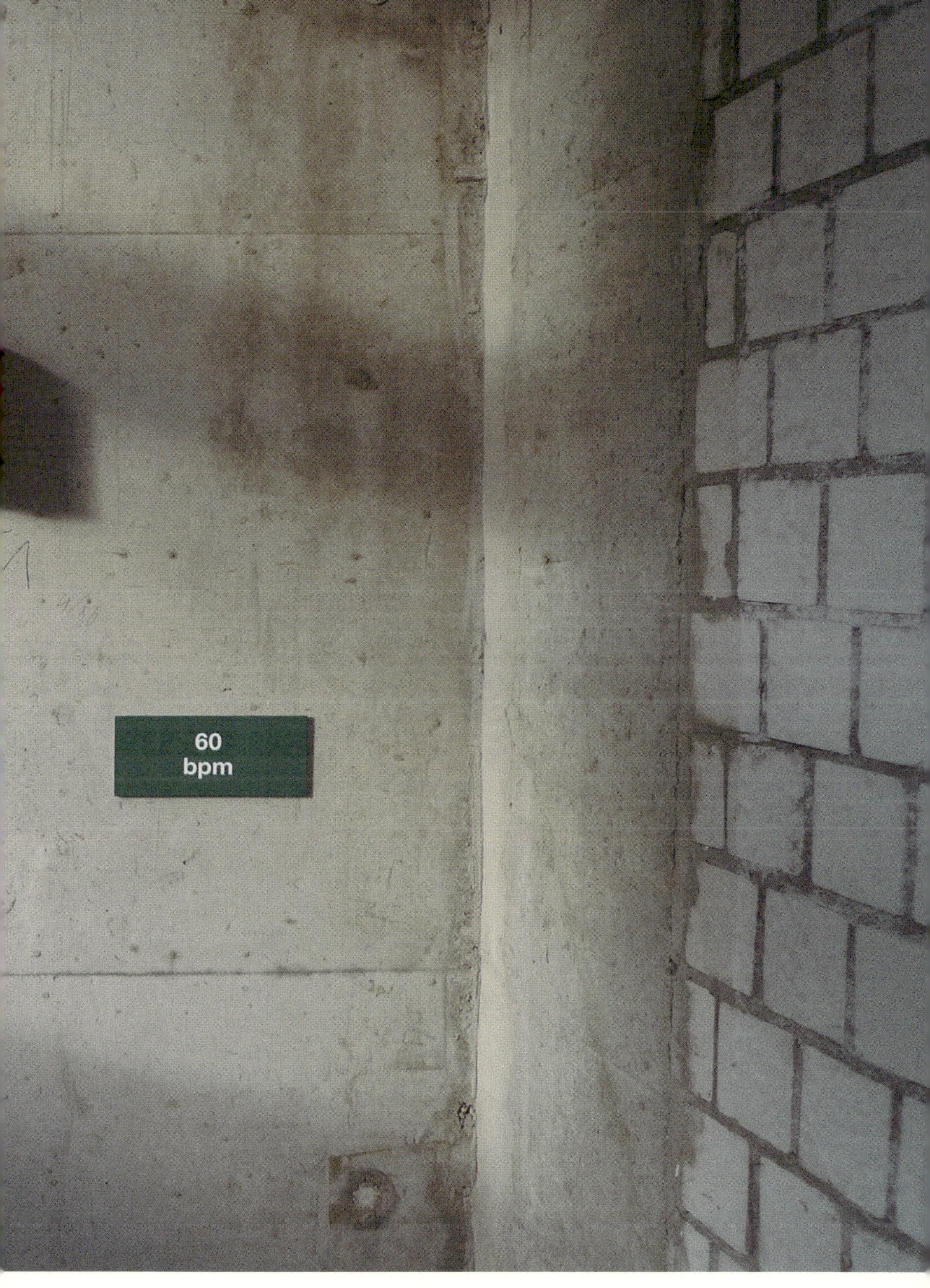
60
bpm

now

now

Captions
and Image Credits

Inside cover:
Ruler Now - End, 2011.
Laser and black paint on
transparent perspex. 24 x 30.4 cm.
Courtesy CE & AKINCI, Amsterdam.
Photo: Peter Cox

pages 10-11
1:86400, 2003.
DVD projection, 1.50 min.
Loop, color, stereo.
Courtesy CE.
Comissioned by ITU (Istanbul
Technical University).

pages 12-13
Graphic notation showing how the
same measure is constructed in two
different ways. Produced for
the booklet of the solo exhibition *Week*
at Kunsthalle Basel, 2012.
Courtesy CE & Kunsthalle Basel.

pages 14-15
Week, 2012
7 grilles from the floor of the Kunsthalle
Oak wood and metal fittings,
48 x 100 x 4.5 cm.
Private collection, Switzerland
Installation view, Kunsthalle Basel.
Courtesy CE and Kunsthalle Basel.
Photo: Serge Hasenböhler
© Kunsthalle Basel, 2012

pages 16-17
Ruler I (Cairo), 2007.
Laser on transparent perspex.
3 x 36 x 0.5 cm.
Courtesy CE & AKINCI, Amsterdam.

pages 18-19
*Sky Ornamentation with
3 Sounding Dots and Anti-Pigeon Net
(SO3SDAPN)*, 2010.
Installation view from the courtyard
of Thyssen-Bornemisza Art Contemporary.
3 directional loud speakers, sound piece,
anti-pigeon net, steel wires.
Sound piece: 40 sec. loop,
3-channel stereo
Courtesy CE.
Commissioned by Thyssen-Bornemisza
Art Contemporary and Vehbi Koç
Foundation.

pages 20-21
Father's Timeline, 2007.
Pencil and marker on paper
50 x 71 cm.
Courtesy Vehbi Koç Foundation.

pages 22-23
Room of Rhythms, 2010–12,
mixed media and architectural additions.
Dimensions variable.
Commissioned and produced
by dOCUMENTA (13) with the support
of SAHA, Istanbul, and the assistance
of MIAM, Istanbul Technical University.
Courtesy CE.
Photo: Rosa Maria Rühling

pages 24-25
Lyrics for *Dark Light Dark*, 2007.
Courtesy CE.

pages 26-27
Installation view from *Room of Rhythms*
at dOCUMENTA (13), 2012.
Mixed media and additional architectural
elements. Dimensions variable.
Photo: Rosa Maria Rühling

pages 28-29
Ruler 0-Now, 2007.
Laser on transparent perspex.
2.5 x 20 x 0.5 cm.
Courtesy CE & AKINCI, Amsterdam.
Photo: Peter Cox

pages 30-31
Sketch for *Time Chart for the
Documenta Worker*, 2012.
Pen, pencil and marker on graph
paper. 21 and 29.7 cm.
Courtesy CE.

page 34:
Sketch for and installation images of *Week*,
Kunsthalle Basel, 2012

page 35
Week, 2012.
Mono sound, 3 min; sound system:
1 folded horn, 2 x 3-way
loudspeakers, 30 band graphic
equalizer, amplifiers, crossover;
white molton; aluminum truss
system; wood.
Courtesy CE and Kunsthalle Basel.
Photo: Serge Hasenböhler
© Kunsthalle Basel, 2012

page 36
Thumbnail 1
View of C&A store, Kassel.

Thumbnail 2
Installation detail from *Room of Rhythms*,
dOCUMENTA (13), 2012.

page 37
Installation view from *Room of Rhythms*
at dOCUMENTA (13), 2012.
Mixed media and architectural additions.
Dimensions variable.
Photo: Rosa Maria Rühling

page 38
Thumbnails 1-2
Kolon, 2010.
Installation view from *Tactics of
Invisibility* at TANAS, Berlin.
Wood construction, plaster, white paint,
4 TV-type loud speakers, 3.27 min loop,
4-channel.
Courtesy CE and Vehbi Koç Foundation.
Commissioned by Thyssen-Bornemisza Art
Contemporary and Vehbi Koç Foundation.

Thumbnail 3
Installation view from *Room of Rhythms*
at dOCUMENTA (13), 2012.
Traffic light beeper (City of Kassel),
button, print on dibond. 1 second loop.
Courtesy CE.

Thumbnail 4
Traffic light beeper in Kassel.

page 39
Kolon, 2011.
Installation view from *Tactics of Invisibility*
at ARTER – Space for Art, Istanbul.
Wood construction, plaster, white paint,
4 TV-type loud speakers, 3.27 min loop,
4-channel.
Courtesy CE and Vehbi Koç Foundation.
Commissioned by Thyssen-Bornemisza Art
Contemporary and Vehbi Koç Foundation.
Photo: Hadiye Cangökçe

page 41
Ruler I (Cairo), 2007.
Laser on transparent perspex. 3 x 36 x 0.5 cm.
Ruler I (Istanbul), 2008.
Laser and black paint on white perspex.
3 x 36 x 0.3 cm.
Ruler I (Antwerp), 2009.
Laser and white paint on transparent
perspex. 2.6 x 37.5 x 0.3 cm.

Installation view of *Rulers
and Rhythm Studies, Untitled
(12th Istanbul Biennial)*, 2011.
Courtesy CE and AKINCI, Amsterdam.
Photo: Özgür Atlağan

page 43
Layout sketch for the first proposal of
this book *Studio*, 2008.
Text by Maxine Kopsa. („Just in Time' –
Proposal for Municipal Art Acquisitions,
curated by Maxine Kopsa, 1.12.06 – 11.03.07,
Stedelijk Museum CS, Amsterdam, NL).
Courtesy CE.

page 45
Ruler 0-Now, 2007.
Laser on transparent perspex.
2.5 x 20 x 0.5 cm.
Courtesy CE & AKINCI, Amsterdam.
Photo: Peter Cox

page 46 thumbnails
Detail from *Day*, 2011.
LED sign, microprocessor.
Courtesy CE and AKINCI, Amsterdam.
Courtesy SALT.
Photo: Refik Anadol

Detail from *Ruler Day Night
(September 2011)*, 2011.
Wood, digital print on white perspex.
100 x 6 x 0.8 cm.
Courtesy CE and AKINCI, Amsterdam.
Photo: Özgür Atlağan

Detail from *Dark Light Dark*, 2007.
Laser and black paint on white perspex.
20 x 2 x 0.3 cm.
Courtesy CE and AKINCI, Amsterdam.

Detail from *Dark Light Dark*, 2007
LED, microprocessor. 110 x 12 x 4 cm.
Courtesy CE and AKINCI, Amsterdam.

page 47
Detail from *Sky Ornamentation with
3 Sounding Dots and Anti-Pigeon Net
(SO3SDAPN)*, 2010.
Site-specific installation.
3 directional loud speakers, sound piece,
anti-pigeon net, steel wires.
Sound piece: 40 sec. loop, 3-channel stereo.
Commissioned by Thyssen-Bornemisza Art
Contemporary and Vehbi Koç Foundation.

page 48
Thumbnail 1
Detail of *Şaşaa*, 2011.
Ornamentation with stickers on
the façade of the building.
Tactics of Invisibility at ARTER
Space for Art, Istanbul.
Commissioned by Thyssen-Bornemisza
Art Contemporary and Vehbi Koç
Foundation.
Courtesy CE and Vehbi Koç Foundation.
Photo © Murat Germen

Thumbnail 2-5
Installation views of *Şaşaa*, 2011.
LED panel, microprocessor.
40 x 8 x 4 cm.
Commissioned by Thyssen-Bornemisza
Art Contemporary and Vehbi Koç
Foundation.
Courtesy CE and Vehbi Koç Foundation.

page 49
View from Variations on the
Rhythms of Room of Rhythms during
the performance, dOCUMENTA (13),
July 13th, 2012.
Photo: Rosa Maria Rühling

pages 50-51
Map, *Room of Rhythms* at
dOCUMENTA (13), 2012.
Drawing and layout: Peer Frantzen
with Cevdet Erek.
Courtesy CE.
Supported by SAHA.

page 53
Map from *SWCS*
(Stedelijk Waterfalls CS) 2006.
Intervention on existing floor plan.
Xerox paper. 21 x 29.7 cm.
Courtesy CE.

page 55
Handout from *4/4 (Nekropsi proudly*
tries), 2007.
Drawing and collage by CE.
Performance by Nekropsi.
Guitars, drums, amplifiers.
Duration: app. 30 min.
Platform Garanti Contemporary
Art Center, Istanbul.

pages 56-56
Façade with cables, Platform Garanti
Contemporary Art Center during
4/4 (Nekropsi proudly tries), 2007.

pages 58-59
Şafak kağıdı (Dawn paper).
Time chart of Turkish soldier.
Free download from
https://ergin53.bildirgec.org/

pages 60-61
Installation view of *Rulers and*
Rhythm Studies, (Untitled)
12th Istanbul Biennial, 2012.
16 Rulers on gray table. 2007–2011.
Rulers from left to right:
Ruler 0 – Now,
Ruler 1 (Cairo),
Ruler 1 (Antwerp),
Ruler 1 (Istanbul),
Ruler 100 Years (with Calendar
and Alphabet Revolution),
Ruler Coup (mini),
Ruler Near (long),
Ruler Near,
Ruler Biennial,
Ruler Rhythm 1,
Circular Week Ruler,
Ruler Day Night (September 2011)
Ruler Now - ,
Ruler Now - End.
Photo: Özgür Atlağan
Installation plan: Elif Akçay

pages 62-63
Day, 2011.
LED sign, microprocessor.
Courtesy CE and AKINCI, Amsterdam.
Courtesy SALT.
Photo: Refik Anadol

Ruler Day Night (September 2011), 2011
Wood, digital print on white perspex.
100 x 6 x 0.8 cm.
Courtesy CE and AKINCI, Amsterdam.
Photo: Özgür Atlağan

Dark Light Dark, panel, 2007.
Laser and black paint on white perspex.
20 x 2 x 0.3 cm.
Courtesy CE and AKINCI, Amsterdam.

Dark Light Dark, LED, 2007.
LED, microprocessor.
110 x 12 x 4 cm.
Courtesy CE and AKINCI, Amsterdam.

page 64
Circular Week Ruler, 2011
Laser and black paint on transparent
perspex. 12 x 12 x 0.3 cm.
Courtesy CE and AKINCI, Amsterdam.
Photo: Peter Cox

page 65
7 & Circular Week Ruler,
Installation view from *Update*,
solo exhibition at AKINCI,
Amsterdam, 2011.
Ruler (see p. 65)
Directional loudspeaker, 00.27 min,
mono, loop 2011.
Courtesy CE and AKINCI, Amsterdam.
Photo: Peter Cox

pages 66-67
Studio, 2005.
Installation view from *Studio*,
Rijksakademie van beeldende kunsten,
Amsterdam.
0.12 min loop, color, mono sound.
Courtesy CE and AKINCI, Amsterdam.
Photo: Roy Taylor

pages 68-69
Ruler Coup (mini), 2011.
Produced in the context of
Untitled (12th Istanbul Biennial).
Edition of 5000.
Ruler Near, 2011. Produced in the
context of Outres mesures et programmes
radio La Galerie Contemporary
Art Center of Noisy-le-Sec.
Edition of 1000.
Photo: Mustafa Hazneci

pages 70-71
Installation view from *Room of Rhythms*
at dOCUMENTA (13).
Photo: Rosa Maria Rühling

page 72
Detail from *Ruler 0-Now*, 2007.

page 75
Detail from *Ruler Now-End*, 2011.

Colophon

This book is published on the occasion of dOCUMENTA (13), Kassel.

This book was realized with the support of the W.F.C. Uriôt prize, awarded to Cevdet Erek during his residency at the Rijksakademie van beeldende kunsten in Amsterdam. For the W.F.C. Uriôt prize an independent jury nominates an artist whose work and work process can be regarded as exceptional and unparalleled.

The *Room of Rhythms* installation is commissioned and produced by dOCUMENTA (13) with the support of SAHA, Istanbul, and the assistance of MIAM, Istanbul Technical University.

© 2012 Cevdet Erek, Duygu Demir and
Verlag der Buchhandlung Walther König, Köln

Editor: Duygu Demir
Copyeditor: Sylee Gore
Design: Sabine Pflitsch (probsteibooks, Cologne)
Production: DZA Druckerei zu Altenburg GmbH

Published by
Verlag der Buchhandlung Walther König, Köln
Ehrenstr. 4, 50672 Köln
Tel. +49 (0) 221 / 20 59 6-53
Fax +49 (0) 221 / 20 59 6-60
verlag@buchhandlung-walther-koenig.de

Bibliographic information published by the Deutsche Nationalbibliothek
The Deutsche Nationalbibliothek lists this publication in the Deutsche
Nationalbibliografie; detailed bibliographic data are available in the Internet
at http://dnb.d-nb.de.

Printed in Germany

Distribution:
Switzerland
AVA Verlagsauslieferungen AG
Centralweg 16, CH-8910 Affoltern a.A.
Tel. +41 (44) 762 42 60
Fax +41 (44) 762 42 10
verlagsservice@ava.ch

UK & Eire
Cornerhouse Publications
70 Oxford Street, GB-Manchester M1 5NH
Fon +44 (0) 161 200 15 03
Fax +44 (0) 161 200 15 04
publications@cornerhouse.org

Outside Europe
D.A.P. / Distributed Art Publishers, Inc.
155 6th Avenue, 2nd Floor, USA-New York, NY 10013
Fon +1 (0) 212 627 1999
Fax +1 (0) 212 627 9484
eleshowitz@dapinc.com

ISBN 978-3-86335-214-1

Ruler *Now – End*, 2011 >